CAREER ESSENTIALS

A PRACTICAL GUIDE TO BUILDING A STRONG FOUNDATION FOR PROFESSIONAL GROWTH

RAHUL MAHESHWARI

Copyright © Rahul Maheshwari 2024
All Rights Reserved.

This book has been self-published with all reasonable efforts taken to make the material error-free by the author. No part of this book shall be used, reproduced in any manner whatsoever without written permission from the author, except in the case of brief quotations embodied in critical articles and reviews.

The Author of this book is solely responsible and liable for its content including but not limited to the views, representations, descriptions, statements, information, opinions and references ["Content"]. The Content of this book shall not constitute or be construed or deemed to reflect the opinion or expression of the Publisher or Editor. Neither the Publisher nor Editor endorse or approve the Content of this book or guarantee the reliability, accuracy or completeness of the Content published herein and do not make any representations or warranties of any kind, express or implied, including but not limited to the implied warranties of merchantability, fitness for a particular purpose. The Publisher and Editor shall not be liable whatsoever for any errors, omissions, whether such errors or omissions result from negligence, accident, or any other cause or claims for loss or damages of any kind, including without limitation, indirect or consequential loss or damage arising out of use, inability to use, or about the reliability, accuracy or sufficiency of the information contained in this book.

Made with ♥ on the Notion Press Platform

www.notionpress.com

The views expressed in this book are solely those of the author and do not reflect the opinions of his current or past employers or educational institutions with which he has been associated.

CONTENTS

PREFACE

Embarking on a career journey is a thrilling and transformative experience. Those initial years in the professional world lay the foundation for a successful career. Yet, this exciting phase can also be bewildering and full of challenges, leaving many young professionals uncertain about their path. That is where this book steps in.

Career Essentials: A Practical Guide to Building a Strong Foundation for Professional Growth is your comprehensive resource, offering actionable insights and strategies for the early stages of your career. In this book, we explore a wide array of topics, encompassing personal attributes, professional skills, and the art of effective interpersonal relationships - vital elements for career success.

Drawing from over one and a half decades of corporate experience, I understand the trials and triumphs that budding professionals encounter. My mission is simple: to share insights, strategies, and practice advice with the next generation of young professionals, enabling them to achieve their career aspirations.

This book is not a run-of-the-mill career guide, brimming with theoretical jargon and far-fetched scenarios. Instead, it is a practical handbook with real-life anecdotes and practical wisdom, handpicked from my personal journey. The book seeks to bridge the mentorship gap that some professionals may encounter in their careers, particularly during the early stages.

The chapters in this book delve into the crucial qualities needed in the early phases of your career, establishing a solid foundation for the future. This is followed by a few case scenarios that you might encounter at some point in your career journey. The case scenarios provide an opportunity to apply some of the concepts covered in this book to real-life situations.

One of the book's highlights is its clear, concise, and practical language, ensuring effortless comprehension for readers. While there are over thirty chapters in the book, they are concrete, supplemented with examples and self-reflection questions. This approach not only throws light on the importance of each concept but also empowers you to apply them in your own professional journeys by providing an opportunity to reflect. If you find it challenging to relate to the self-reflection questions in the nascent stage of your career, do not worry; they will become increasingly valuable when you revisit them as you progress in your professional journey.

The concepts outlined in this book, if practiced diligently and consistently, will enable you to position yourself as an asset for your leaders, managers, peers, and clients alike. By implementing the practical advice and strategies outlined in these pages, you will not only enhance your professional capabilities but also be appreciated and sought after by those around you.

The book aims to serve you not only as a one-time read but as a constant companion - a ready reckoner and reference - for you to review repeatedly, as you navigate and progress through the various stages of your career. Consider it a reliable guide that evolves with you, offering insights and guidance whenever you need them in your professional journey.

Career Essentials: A Practical Guide to Building a Strong Foundation for Professional Growth is an indispensable tool for anyone setting out on their career path. Filled with real-world examples and pragmatic guidance, it equips readers with the confidence and strategies needed to navigate the professional realm and achieve their career aspirations. I hope this book becomes a cherished resource as you embark on your own career journey.

INTRODUCTION

TRANSITION FROM COLLEGE TO CORPORATE

Our journey through life encompasses unique phases that significantly influence our thinking, choices, and actions. In our formative years, our survival is deeply dependent on care provided by parents or guardians. In early childhood, we frequently adhere to guidance from our elders. With the maturation of our cognitive abilities, we gradually assume more autonomy in decision-making. As we progress into secondary education, our thoughts become increasingly shaped by teachers and peers. Upon entering college, the influence of our peers tends to reach its peak and holds substantial influence over our lives.

For many of us, college life holds a pivotal role in shaping our future, laying the groundwork for what lies ahead. It is during this phase that we embrace a newfound sense of autonomy, often living away from our parents or guardians, and making independent decisions. We select our friends, participate in enjoyable activities, venture into uncharted territories, and cultivate experiences that leave a lasting imprint in our memories. As college draws to a close, a sense of anticipation often arises as we eagerly look forward to embarking on our professional journey, be it through campus placements, off-campus placements, or other avenues.

Upon graduating from college, the transition to professional world commences, signifying an exciting and satisfying phase as it signifies the first major step towards financial independence. Gainful employment empowers us to earn and manage our finances according to our preferences while contributing to a purpose. Remarkably, work plays a substantial role in our lives, with statistics indicating that individuals, on average, dedicate more than a third of their entire lifespan, equivalent to around 90,000 hours, to their careers.

While college life and early career are both special in their own ways, the successful shift from college to the corporate world is a critical aspect. It is common for individuals to have a multitude of questions running through their minds during this transition. Here is a quick take on what the transition from college to campus could look like.

In college, the focus is primarily on academic pursuits, personal growth, and exploration. Students navigate a flexible schedule, engaging in a variety of courses to broaden their knowledge. The emphasis is on individual learning, collaboration with peers on projects and assignments, and a sense of autonomy in managing one's time and priorities. Social interactions are often informal, and the environment fosters a sense of community and shared experiences.

On the other hand, corporate life introduces a shift in focus towards professional responsibilities, teamwork, and achieving organizational goals. The structured nature of a corporate setting typically comes with defined roles, hierarchical structures, and a clear delineation of tasks. Employees often work within specific departments, collaborating on projects that contribute to the company's success. Time management becomes more structured, with deliverables and deadlines playing a crucial role. The corporate environment also introduces formal communication channels, professional etiquette, and a corporate culture that emphasizes productivity and efficiency.

When a college graduate joins an organization, they can expect to go through an overall onboarding and training program that is specifically designed to help them integrate into the company and its culture. This generally includes learning about the company's mission, vision, values, and goals, as well as its policies, procedures, and different departments in the organization. They are generally also introduced to the company's products or services and trained on the tools and technologies used within the organization to support clients.

Once the overall organization level onboarding is complete, the new employees are assigned to teams in which they will be working on a day-to-day basis. The team may have its own onboarding process specific to its projects. It would also involve on-the-job training (learning while working) and job shadowing (supporting another team member for learning purposes).

The manager will typically give new joiners an understanding of what their job responsibilities are and what they are expected to accomplish. They will get a sense of how their performance will be evaluated and what metrics or targets they need to achieve. They may also get a view of how their role fits into the broader goals of the organization. If you are not explicitly briefed about some of the aspects described above, ask your manager to help you understand these better.

New joiners can expect to collaborate with colleagues and supervisors to complete tasks and projects assigned to them. They may be given guidance and feedback on their work and expected to continuously learn and improve their skills. They may also have opportunities for professional development, such as attending trainings or workshops, and participating in mentorship or coaching programs. They will have a plan and objectives in place which focuses on their career growth and development. A development plan, usually created by employees themselves and discussed with their manager, will have details on where the employee wants to be in the next few years based on their aspirations and an action plan with well-defined milestones on how they can get there.

During college years, the main objective is to study, acquire knowledge, and achieve excellent grades in examinations. However, when we enter the corporate world, the primary focus shifts to the customer, and meeting and exceeding customer expectations. The customer is the reason any organization exists, and without customers, there is no need for an organization. Consequently, most decisions and actions taken by individuals or groups within an organization should revolve around the customer.

The transition from the more fluid and exploratory college life to the structured and goal-oriented corporate life is a significant adjustment that individuals navigate as they enter the workforce.

SKILL REQUIREMENT BY CAREER STAGE

While the skills needed in each of the early career phases may vary by organization, this book emphasizes elements that are universally applicable, regardless of the industry or organization. Consider the expectations that we hold as consumers - prompt response, efficient delivery, and top-notch quality from service providers. These are the same standards our customers will inevitably hold us to. Despite the ever-evolving landscape of business, these expectations remain remarkably constant. Customers consistently seek improved products and services delivered swiftly and at reasonable prices. Conversely, they are unhappy with tardy delivery, overpriced goods and services lacking value, or substandard quality. Amidst the dynamic nature of the business world, it is reassuring to have identified these constant factors, which serve as guiding principles for professional success.

Similarly, organizations and managers have consistent expectations of their employees, irrespective of the industry or job type. These expectations encompass qualities such as curiosity, adaptability, commitment to quality, proficiency in communication, collaboration, and problem-solving. Even if not expressly articulated, there is often an implicit expectation for employees to demonstrate these behaviors.

Surpassing both explicit and implicit expectations can distinguish you from your peers, establishing a robust groundwork for your career. Demonstrating these behaviors proactively, without explicit instructions, enhances your professionalism and further sets you apart. Consistently integrating these traits into your actions can help you cultivate habits that serve as catalysts for your long-term career growth.

There are additional elements that are typically not explicitly expected of an individual but practicing these can enhance one's professional journey and pave the way for long-term success. These include effective understanding of the organization culture, time management, building a strong professional network, and having a mentor to guide you in your career. In the book, we will discuss the topics that, if given good attention to, can help you establish a sturdy base for a prosperous career. These can broadly be classified into three categories:

Professional Skills - Professional skills are job-specific competencies and knowledge that contribute to success in a particular field or industry. Technical skills, such as programming are critical in roles that require specialized expertise. Industry-specific knowledge involves understanding regulations, staying informed about trends, and developing domain-specific expertise. Analytical skills, including critical thinking and problem-solving, enhance the ability to make informed decisions. Certifications, qualifications, and continuous learning contribute to professional development. Networking, strategic thinking, and proficiency in managing portfolios of projects are essential for career advancement, highlighting the importance of a well-rounded professional skill set.

Personal Attributes - Personal attributes refer to individual qualities that contribute to effective self-management and personal well-being. These skills encompass aspects such as adaptability, emotional intelligence, creativity and innovation, integrity, and having a positive mindset. These skills collectively contribute to forming the foundation for personal growth and resilience.

Interpersonal Skills - Interpersonal skills are necessary for effective communication and collaboration with others. Communication skills, including verbal and written communication, active listening, and presentation abilities, are crucial for conveying information clearly and building relationships. Teamwork and collaboration involve working harmoniously with colleagues, resolving conflicts, and networking to create a positive and cooperative work environment.

In the chapters that follow, we will dive deeper into these skills understanding why they are important, how we can develop them, and self-reflect on each of these. But before we get there, let us touch upon an organization's typical structure and your potential stakeholders within the organization. This would be particularly relevant for those who have not had an exposure of the corporate world yet.

ORGANIZATION STRUCTURE AND STAKEHOLDERS

Simply put, an organization is an ecosystem where various departments, teams, and individuals work together and depend on each other to achieve common goals. Like a natural ecosystem, an organization has its own dynamics, interrelationships, and dependencies, where the success of one element affects the entire system. The flow of information, resources, and communication within the organization creates a complex network of interactions and feedback loops that determine the overall health and effectiveness of the organization. The specific departments in an organization can vary depending on the nature of the organization and its goals. However, some common departments in most organizations along with a simplistic view of their function are listed below:

i. **Research and Development (R&D)** - The R&D department is responsible for researching and developing new products, services, or technologies that the organization can offer to customers.

ii. **Operations** - The operations department is responsible for managing the day-to-day activities of the organization, including production, logistics, and supply chain management.

iii. **Sales** - The sales department is responsible for selling the organization's products or services to customers and developing and maintaining relationships with them.

iv. **Marketing** - The marketing department is responsible for promoting the organization's products or services to potential customers, as well as maintaining and improving the organization's brand reputation.

v. **Finance** - The finance department is responsible for managing the financial operations of the organization, including accounting, budgeting, financial analysis, and financial reporting.

vi. **Human Resources (HR)** - The HR department is responsible for managing people-related matters, including hiring, training, payroll, benefits administration, and employee relations. Many organizations, in the recent past, have renamed this department to use a terminology that emphasizes 'people' rather than 'resources,' to avoid viewing employees as mere resources.

vii. **Information Technology (IT)** - The IT department is responsible for managing the organization's computer systems and technology infrastructure, including hardware, software, networks, and security.

viii. **Customer Service** - The customer service department is responsible for providing support to customers, including answering questions, resolving issues, and providing product or service information.

ix. **Legal & Regulatory** - The legal department is responsible for ensuring that the organization follows laws and regulations, as well as providing legal advice and support to the organization's management.

x. **Environmental, Social, and Governance (ESG)** - The ESG department in an organization is responsible for managing and implementing strategies related to sustainability, social responsibility, and corporate governance. This department focuses on ensuring the company's operations align with ethical and responsible business practices, encompassing environmental impact, social initiatives, and governance structures.

Please note that department names can vary between companies, and your organization may have additional departments based on its specific needs. Regardless of the name, each department plays a critical role in the success of an organization, and effective collaboration and communication among departments is key to achieving organization's goals.

While an organization will have multiple departments, within your own department you will have a primary set of stakeholders who will typically be related to you and your work:

1. **Your manager** - Your manager will be one of your key stakeholders. Your work, good or bad, directly impacts them. Ensure that you understand their expectations and clearly grasp their objectives to work towards achieving them. Avoid doing something that puts your manager in a bad light.

2. **Your manager's manager** - Your manager's manager is also someone who cares about how well you do your job and what you bring to the team and function. They look at the big picture for the organization and might check on how well the team and everyone are doing. They expect you to work well, be productive, and collaborate with others. Since they will mostly have an influence in determining your performance, it is crucial to have a good relationship with them and meet their expectations for your career to progress.

3. **Your manager's peers** - Your managers' peers are colleagues who hold similar management positions as your manager. You may collaborate with them on some projects outside of your team. As you interact and collaborate with them, your performance will shape their perception of you. Ensure that while working with your manager's peers, you give your best to shine and earn respect not just for yourself but also your team and manager. Your manager's peers may also impact your opportunities for advancement within the organization, so building positive relationships with them becomes important for career growth. They can also provide valuable insights and perspectives to improve your skills and knowledge, so be receptive to their feedback.

4. **Your team/team members** - The way you collaborate with other team members will determine team dynamics.

If you are willing to help your team members and share what you have learned and best practices with them, it will create a positive team environment. Over time, a team can build a reputation for itself for being very cohesive and be a role model for other teams. If you build good relationships with your team members, you can also interact informally with them, on professional and personal matters, and build a strong support system for yourself.

5. **Your customers** - Customers are generally also referred to as clients. Your customers are a direct beneficiary of your work. They are important stakeholders for you because they are the source of revenue for your organization as well as the reason for your organization's existence. Customers provide feedback on the quality of products or services that you provide to them that will directly impact your performance and growth. A satisfied customer can become a loyal customer, refer others to the organization, and provide positive reviews and testimonials, which can benefit you and your organization's reputation, top line, and bottom line. You will also feel fulfilled by serving your customers well.

6. **Others** - Depending on your role, there may be other stakeholders like team members from other functions, vendors or suppliers, regulators, community, shareholders etc. who you may need to collaborate with depending on the nature of your work.

Now that you have a hang of what an organization is structured like, and who could be your key stakeholders in the organization, let us get into the details of what it would entail to have a solid foundation for a successful career.

1.

DECIPHERING ORGANIZATIONAL LANDSCAPE

Deciphering organizational landscape implies understanding multiple aspects of an organization including its brand, positioning, financials, social initiatives, and much more. However, I will restrict this chapter to only a few fundamental elements like an organization's vision, mission, values, culture, and dynamics.

Navigating the corporate world can be daunting, especially for those new to the workforce or have recently joined an organization. Understanding the workplace landscape is crucial for success in the corporate world. A few elements of the organizational landscape are discussed below.

VISION

Vision is a forward-looking statement that describes the aspirational future state the organization aims to achieve. It is a motivational guide, inspiring and aligning employees and stakeholders toward a shared long-term goal. A well-crafted vision is often concise, and memorable, and paints a picture of what success looks like for the organization. An example of a vision statement is 'To be the global leader in sustainable innovation, providing solutions for a better and greener world.'

MISSION

Mission outlines the organization's core purpose, specifying what it does, who it serves, and how it adds value. It clarifies the fundamental reason for the organization's existence and provides a foundation for strategic decision-making. A mission statement is typically more detailed than a vision, covering the present and the organization's immediate focus. An example of a mission statement is 'To deliver high-quality, affordable healthcare solutions to communities worldwide, improving lives and fostering well-being.'

How will you benefit from having a good understanding of your organization's vision and mission?

i. **Strategic career planning** - A strong understanding of the organization's vision and mission allows you to strategically plan your career growth. You can identify areas for skill development and seek projects that align with both your personal and organizational goals.

ii. **Meaningful contribution** - When you understand and connect with the organization's vision and mission, you find a deeper sense of purpose in your work. This intrinsic motivation contributes to higher job satisfaction and engagement, as you would be able to see how your efforts contribute to the bigger picture.

iii. **Team motivation and engagement** - If you have clarity on your organization's vision and mission, you can communicate and provide the same clarity to your team, particularly when you get into a team lead or manager role. This will help keep your team motivated and engaged.

iv. **Shared values** - The vision and mission often reflect the values that the organization upholds. This alignment is essential for your satisfaction and well-being, as working in an environment that resonates with your values fosters a positive and fulfilling professional experience.

Understanding an organization's vision and mission functions like a compass, guiding individuals toward a shared purpose, making every step count.

Example

Here is an example illustrating the connection to the organization's purpose. While a person supporting a pharmaceutical company in generating sales force reports may see their role as primarily involving number-crunching and email communications, a broader perspective reveals significant impact. These reports, seemingly routine, play a pivotal role in guiding pharmaceutical representatives to visit the 'right' doctors at the 'right' time, using the 'right' communication channels, and with the 'right' frequency. Consequently, this strategic approach ensures that doctors receive the 'right' information needed to administer the 'right' treatment to patients, directly influencing patient lives. Recognizing this relationship between the report and its impact on patients may not be immediately apparent without considering the larger context or the "big picture." However, once realized, this will provide significant meaning to the work that one is doing, transforming routine tasks into impactful contributions to the organization's overarching mission.

As you embark on your professional journey, understanding the vision and mission of an organization becomes more than just a corporate mantra - it becomes your guiding light. By aligning your goals with the broader vision and contributing to the mission, you not only enhance the organization's trajectory but carve out a purposeful path for yourself.

CULTURE AND DYNAMICS

Organizational culture refers to the shared values, beliefs, and behaviors of an organization. It can include things like dress code, communication styles, work hours, and even the physical layout of the office. Understanding and adapting to workplace culture is important for fitting in with the overall organizational culture. If the culture of the organization does not align with your values, it is likely that you will not enjoy working there.

Company culture is not just a buzzword; it's the heartbeat of success. Tune into it, understand it, and let it guide your rhythm.

Dynamics in the workplace can refer to the relationships between colleagues and superiors, power structures, and team dynamics.

Organizational culture and dynamics play a significant role in shaping how individuals communicate and work together within an organization. Failing to adapt to the culture of an organization can lead to misunderstandings, conflicts, and poor job performance. If an organization has a culture that values direct communication and quick decision-making, individuals who prefer to communicate indirectly and take more time to make decisions may struggle to fit in. This can result in misunderstandings, frustration, and ultimately, poor job performance. Similarly, if an organization has a hierarchical power structure, individuals who prefer a more egalitarian work environment may struggle to adapt and feel undervalued or unheard. Understanding and adapting to organizational culture and dynamics is crucial for effective communication, teamwork, and job performance.

Examples

An example of a disconnect between an individual's value system and an organization's culture could be a person who values work-life balance but works for a company that promotes a culture of working long hours and prioritizing work over personal time. Another example is if you have a strong ethical code and believe in doing what is right, but your company culture is more focused on cut-throat competition and can compromise on integrity (e.g., encouraging bribery) to gain more profits. In either of the cases, you may find it difficult to align with the organization's values and may struggle with ethical dilemmas in your work.

An example of workplace dynamics is the relationship between managers and their subordinates. Managers have a significant impact on the work environment and how employees feel about their jobs. If a manager is supportive, respectful, and values their employees' input, it can create a positive and productive workplace culture. On the other hand, if a manager is harsh, unapproachable, and dismisses employee concerns, it can create a negative and demotivating work environment. This dynamic can affect employee morale, job satisfaction, and overall productivity.

Another example of workplace dynamics is the relationship between different teams or departments within an organization. For instance, in an organization that provided analytics services to customers, there was tension between two teams because they were targeting the same customer for the same service to meet their individual revenue targets. This led to conflicts and lack of cooperation that affected the overall performance of the organization. Effective workplace dynamics in this case would require the teams to have a clear understanding of each other's roles, responsibilities and goals, and to find ways to collaborate and support each other for the overall success of the organization.

How will you benefit from having a good understanding of organization culture and dynamics?

i. **Stronger relationships** - Understanding organization culture and knowing how to navigate organization dynamics can help you build strong relationships with co-workers, communicate effectively with superiors, and contribute to a positive and productive team environment.

ii. **Better career prospects** - Understanding the culture and dynamics of your organization can better equip you to navigate its structure and identify opportunities for career advancement.

iii. **Improved communication** - If you understand the company culture and dynamics, you will be able to communicate more meaningfully with your colleagues and managers, leading to more effective collaboration and problem-solving.

iv. **Higher job satisfaction** - Settling well into organization culture can make you feel at ease. You would be able to see if the culture is aligned to your values. If so, you and the organization could be a good fit for each other, and you will feel satisfied.

How can you better understand the company landscape?

Some tips for navigating the corporate world and understanding company landscape are:

i. **Read company materials** - You can visit the company website and review the company's mission and vision statements, values, and employee handbook to gain a better understanding of its culture. You can also refer to company policies on various matters like finance, people, and learning and training.

ii. **Talk to current/past employees** - You can speak with current or former employees, to understand the company's culture and dynamics. If you have your college seniors or peers already working in the same organization, connecting with them can yield you the best and unfiltered information about organizational culture and dynamics.

iii. **Observe and learn** - If company culture and dynamics are not much talked about explicitly, pay attention to your environment and observe how colleagues and superiors interact with each other. This can help you understand the unwritten rules and expectations of the organization.

iv. **Utilize online review platforms** - There are certain websites which provide employee reviews and insights into company culture. While individual experiences may vary, these platforms can offer a general sense of employee engagement and satisfaction.

SUMMARY

In conclusion, understanding the intricate landscape of an organization is fundamental for success in the corporate world. This chapter delved into elements such as the organization's vision, mission, values, culture, and dynamics. These components serve as guiding principles that shape decision-making, behavior, and interactions within the workplace.

By comprehending and aligning with the organization's vision and mission, you can strategically plan your career growth and find deeper purpose in your work. By embracing a holistic understanding of the organizational landscape, you can navigate the complexities of the corporate world with clarity and purpose. This not only fosters your personal growth and fulfilment but also contributes to the overall success of the organization.

Self-Reflection

i. *What do I know about my organization's culture and dynamics? What steps would I take to understand them better?*

ii. *How are my organization's values aligned with my values?*

iii. *What is my organization's vision and mission? How do I see myself contributing to my organization's vision and mission?*

2.

MASTERING LEARNING AGILITY

Learning agility is the ability and willingness to learn and adapt quickly in new and unfamiliar situations. It involves being open to new experiences, seeking out challenges, and being willing to take risks and learn from failure. Learning agile individuals can process new information quickly and apply it to solve problems, make decisions, and take action. They are also able to apply their past experiences and knowledge to new situations and learn from feedback to continuously improve their performance. Learning agility is a highly valued skill in the workplace as it allows individuals to stay adaptable and responsive to changing business needs and demands.

Example

I have observed fresh graduates who made substantial contributions to their teams within three months of joining an organization. These individuals were highly dedicated, motivated, and eager to learn. Conversely, there were those who took up to a year to reach their full potential. The sooner you engage with projects and autonomously deliver results, the more promising your short-term prospects will be. When it comes to exploring diverse work areas, some individuals are enthusiastic about continuously learning new domains, while others prefer to specialize in one. In initial stages of your career, you are typically expected to focus on a specific area and make a meaningful impact in that area. Once you have gained proficiency, expressing your interest in learning, and contributing to other areas becomes viable. If you are interested in contributing outside of your own area of work, you may be required to invest extra hours beyond the organization's official expectations, to do justice to your existing role while working on another project to gain new experience or acquire new skills.

How does it help to have good learning agility at the workplace?

i.   **Better knowledge** - The more you learn, the more knowledgeable you become. If you are learning and building knowledge in one area or domain, you are on your way to become a subject matter expert in that area.

ii. **Continuous improvement** - Learning agile individuals are continuously seeking opportunities to improve their skills and knowledge. They take on new challenges and tasks, embrace feedback, and seek out learning opportunities. You can keep adding value to yourself if you are an agile learner.

iii. **Gain recognition** - If you can make a positive contribution to team or function in a short period of time, you gain recognition and respect from your colleagues, manager, and leadership.

iv. **Faster growth** - Learning and being able to deliver positive impact quickly will typically lead to a faster career growth for you.

v.   **Need of the hour** – With the rapidly changing technological landscape, for example, advances in GenAI tools, it becomes imperative that you keep yourselves updated with latest developments in this area and how you could leverage it to enhance your productivity.

What can impede learning agility?

i.   **Fixed mindset** - A fixed mindset can hinder learning agility as it involves the belief that intelligence and abilities are fixed traits that cannot be changed. Individuals with a fixed mindset may be less likely to take on new challenges and may give up more easily when faced with difficulties.

ii. **Fear of failure** - Fear of failure can prevent individuals from taking risks and trying new things, which can hinder learning agility. People who are afraid of failure may be less likely to seek out new experiences or challenges and may avoid situations where they may not be immediately successful.

iii. **Lack of curiosity** - Curiosity is an important trait for learning agility, as it involves a willingness to explore new ideas and ask questions. A lack of curiosity can prevent individuals from seeking out new learning opportunities and may cause them to be less engaged and motivated in their work.

iv. **Resistance to change** - Resistance to change can hinder learning agility as it involves a reluctance to embrace new ideas or ways of doing things. Individuals who are resistant to change may struggle to adapt to new situations or may be less likely to seek out new learning opportunities.

v.   **Lack of feedback** - Feedback is essential for learning and growth, and a lack of feedback can hinder learning agility. Individuals who do not receive regular feedback may struggle to identify areas for improvement and may be less likely to seek out new learning opportunities.

How can you develop and demonstrate learning agility?

i.   **Observe others** - Be a keen observer and learn on how others who have already been in the organization for some times are approaching projects or problems. Add your perspective to it to see if you can do even better when you get a chance. While learning happens best with your own experiences, learning by observing others can be your next best option.

ii. **Be open to learning** - If you find something difficult to understand, ask questions to clarify your doubts. If you require additional hands-on practice to better comprehend something, be willing to do it. During the onboarding process, if you need more time than a full working day to complete pieces of training and assigned tasks, be open to invest that extra time to expedite your learning and be productive faster.

iii. **Learn from diverse sources** - To become a well-rounded learner, you need to learn from a variety of sources. This includes formal training, on-the-job experiences, mentoring, coaching, and self-directed learning. You can seek out different learning opportunities to build a diverse set of skills and knowledge.

iv. **Embrace unfamiliar situations** - Try getting into unfamiliar situations. Staying within your comfort zone minimizes discomfort and struggle, but it also means missing out on the potential growth and performance boost. In the end, you will remain largely unchanged, and the value of the new experience will be lost.

v. **Take calculated risks** - Taking on new challenges allows you to develop new skills and perspectives that may become an important part of your repertoire in the future. Even if something goes wrong and impacts you adversely, take it as a learning for the future which you had no other way to get. For most of us, there will be no one to tell us this - *you can take more calculated risks at the start of your career than at later stages.* Try avoiding the natural inclination to 'play safe,' even when you can potentially take some calculated risks.

vi. **Explore additional solutions** - When you are working on a problem, do not restrict yourself to the first solution that comes to mind. You can explore alternative solutions that have not been considered before. Consider what is making you choose this solution and ask yourself, *"if I didn't have these constraints, how would I have approached this problem?"*

vii. **Experiment with different approaches** - To be a good learner, you need to experiment with different approaches to problem-solving. Instead of sticking to one approach, try new methods and techniques to see what works best for you. This can help you become more versatile and adaptable in the face of new challenges.

viii. **Develop a growth mindset** - Learning agility requires a growth mindset - the belief that your abilities and intelligence can be developed through hard work and dedication. Individuals with a growth mindset are more resilient in the face of setbacks and failures and are more likely to take risks and try new things.

ix. **Stay updated** - Learning agility requires staying up to date with the latest trends, technologies, and industry developments. You can read industry publications, attend conferences, and participate in online forums to stay updated and informed.

x. **Practice reflection** - Learning agile individuals regularly reflect on their experiences and learn from them. You can take time to reflect on your performance, identify what worked well and what could be improved, and set goals for future learning and development.

Learning is not a destination; it is a journey. Be agile and adaptable and thrive in the continuous evolution of knowledge.

SUMMARY

To summarize, this chapter underscored the pivotal role of adaptability and continuous learning in shaping your career trajectory. By observing, learning from others, and adding your unique insights to the experiences of seasoned colleagues, you lay the groundwork for accelerated growth. Embracing diverse learning sources and venturing beyond your comfort zone will enable you to cultivate versatility and resilience in the face of challenges.

Moreover, fostering a growth mindset empowers you to view setbacks as stepping stones to success and to seize calculated risks for professional advancement. Finally, staying informed about industry trends and reflecting on your experiences ensures that you remain agile and relevant in an ever-evolving landscape. Armed with these strategies, you embark on a journey of lifelong learning and career fulfilment, equipped to navigate the complexities of the modern workplace with confidence and agility.

Self-Reflection

i. *When was the last time I learnt and used a new skill? How long did I take to learn it? How could I have accelerated my learning?*

ii. *How do I stay updated on industry trends and advancements in my field?*

3.

BUILDING TECHNICAL AND FUNCTIONAL SKILLS

In a fast-paced, technology-driven work environment, technical skills have become more critical than ever before, as companies increasingly rely on technology to streamline processes, improve productivity, and stay competitive. These technical skills could range from computer or cloud applications to programming languages.

Functional skills, on the other hand, are job-specific competencies that include a good understanding of how the business operates, what the processes are in the industry or an organization, how the data and information flows across systems, business rules used to compute certain key metrics, etc. Functional skills are important in the workplace as they enable an employee to perform their job responsibilities efficiently and effectively. Functional skills will vary significantly with the domain or industry e.g., skills required for a human resource professional, a financial professional, an FMCG (Fast Moving Consumer Goods) professional and a software professional will be vastly different.

Depending on the industry, new employees are expected to pick on technical and functional skills. They are typically imparted these skills through a specially designed onboarding and training program. The program may include training sessions, quizzes, and assessments, and in some cases, hands-on 'dummy projects. These activities are used to evaluate how prepared the individual is to perform on a real-life project.

After the completion of training, a tenured colleague typically provides the new employee with knowledge transfer, which is also known as 'KT' in business parlance. The objective of KT is to transition project knowledge to new team member so that they can effectively and independently work on the project. With the advancement in technology, these KT sessions can be recorded for documentation purposes and can also serve as a point of reference for the new employee in the future. At times, the new employee may be requested to present their comprehension of the project and business understanding to the person who had provided the knowledge. This is done to evaluate if the new employee has grasped and internalized the knowledge correctly. Any gaps in knowledge and understanding discovered at this stage can be addressed in subsequent KT sessions.

Organizations expect employees to be an expert in either a technical area or a functional area or a combination of both depending on the requirement. Having strong technical and/or functional skills can help an employee to be more productive and contribute more effectively to the overall goals of the organization.

Equip yourself with the tools of expertise, for in the world of careers, skills are your strongest currency.

Example

In one of my previous organizations, new associates who joined the organization were made to undergo a functional training to equip them to deliver projects and serve customers. The training was followed by an assessment to evaluate the understanding and application of concepts. It ensured that anyone new joining the organization had the same, good understanding of the functional aspects. Similarly, depending on the team the associate joined, they were made to undertake technical trainings. This could be in ETL (extract-transform-load) technologies, BI (Business Intelligence) technologies or advanced analytics like AI & ML skills based on team and project requirements.

What are the benefits of gaining technical and functional expertise?

i. **Meet expectations** - For some teams, gaining technical and functional expertise is a basic minimum requirement for effectively delivering in the role. Failing to acquire and use these skills could lead to missing expectations from the role.

ii. **Increased confidence** - As a new joiner becomes more proficient in their job duties, their confidence will increase. They will be more willing to take on new tasks and challenges, which can lead to personal and professional growth.

iii. **Improved efficiency** - With technical expertise, a new joiner can perform their job more efficiently. They will be able to use their knowledge to complete tasks and projects with greater ease, which can help increase their productivity.

iv. **Career advancement** - Gaining technical and functional expertise can also help a new joiner to advance in their career. By acquiring new skills and knowledge, they can take on more challenging roles and responsibilities within the organization.

v. **Better communication** - Technical and functional expertise can also improve communication with colleagues and stakeholders. With a better understanding of the technical and functional aspects of the job, team members can communicate more effectively with each other, customers, and other stakeholders by understanding them better as well as talking a language that is easier for them to understand.

How can one build technical or functional skills?

i. **Complete trainings diligently** - Many organizations provide training programs for employees to learn new technical or functional skills. These could be in the form of workshops, webinars, or online courses. These are a huge investment from the organization for you. So, complete the pre-work if any, attend these trainings and take advantage of these opportunities to build your skills, even if it gets a little overwhelming at times.

ii. **Shadow a colleague** - Find a colleague who is an expert in the area you want to develop skills in and ask if you can observe and assist them. This will give you firsthand experience and allow you to learn from someone who has already mastered the skills.

iii. **Practice on your own** - Identify areas where you need to improve and practice on your own time. This could involve working on projects outside of your regular duties or experimenting with new software or tools.

iv. **Get feedback** - Seek feedback from your colleagues or supervisor on your work. This will help you identify areas where you need to improve and how.

v. **Pursue courses** - Formal education, courses and trainings can provide a solid foundation for technical and functional skills. You can pursue a degree or certification program in your field of interest or attend workshops and training sessions to expand your knowledge and skills. Pursuing courses today is easier than ever before with a plethora of online platforms providing certification or degree courses from reputed universities and organizations. However, do assess the value that the course offers before you enrol in it.

SUMMARY

To summarize, navigating the modern career landscape demands a multifaceted approach that encompasses both technical and functional expertise. As organizations increasingly rely on technology to drive efficiency and innovation, proficiency in software applications, programming languages, and other technical skills has become paramount. Simultaneously, a deep understanding of industry processes, data flows, and business rules is essential for effective execution of job responsibilities. Through dedicated training programs, mentorship opportunities, and a commitment to lifelong learning, you can cultivate the skills needed to meet organizational expectations, enhance efficiency, and pave the way for your career advancement. The pursuit of technical and functional expertise is not only advisable but imperative if you strive to excel in your professional journey.

Self-Reflection

i. *How am I fulfilling the demands of my organization for current requirements of functional and technical skills?*

ii. *What are the skills that I believe will be needed in the future and I need to focus on?*

4.

PURSUING QUALITY EXCELLENCE

A product or service is said to be of 'good' quality if it meets or exceeds customer expectations. Quality is of utmost importance in the workplace as it has a direct impact on the reputation, success, and profitability of an organization.

While we all understand the importance of quality, while using products and services in our daily life, we frequently come across sub-optimal products or service experiences. Before delving deep into the topic of quality, let us consider a few *"pizza"* scenarios, and think of how you would feel in each of them.

Scenario 1: Let us say you order a pizza at your home from a nearby restaurant. However, when you open the box to have the pizza, it does not have the toppings that you had ordered. How would you feel?

Most likely, receiving a pizza without the toppings that were ordered will be frustrating and disappointing for you. It will lead to a negative experience and impact the overall satisfaction with the product and the company providing it.

Scenario 2: What if you had ordered a thin-crust wheat base pizza but got a cheese burst one?

If you ordered a thin crust wheat base pizza and received a cheese burst, you will most likely feel furious, disappointed, or upset, especially if you have dietary restrictions or preferences. Even if the restaurant accepts a return or provides a replacement, you will be frustrated to an extent that you will likely reject the offer and ask for a refund. In your mind, you would rather place the order with another restaurant.

Scenario 3: How would you feel if there were wrong deliveries for two consecutive orders from the same restaurant?

You will surely feel frustrated and utterly disappointed with the service. You may also feel like your time and money have been wasted, especially if you had to wait a long time for the delivery. Additionally, you will begin to lose trust in the company and start considering alternative options.

Scenario 4: Would it matter if those two consecutive incorrect orders were delivered by two different people?

From a customer's perspective, it would not matter if the two deliveries were made by two different people. You perhaps would still be dissatisfied with the service and the quality of the deliveries. As a customer, your focus is on the end result, which is the delivery, and not on who made the mistake or what caused it. Therefore, it is important for a company to have systems and processes in place to ensure quality and accuracy in every delivery, regardless of who is working on it.

I trust that the examples provided above illustrate the significance of quality and its potential influence on customer experience. Although the instances revolve around food delivery, the sentiments hold true for any customer encountering subpar quality in products or services in any industry.

What are the advantages of maintaining quality of your products and services?

i. **Higher customer satisfaction** - Good quality products or services lead to higher levels of customer satisfaction, which in turn can lead to repeat business, positive word-of-mouth referrals and higher revenue.

ii. **Improved efficiency** - Good quality work reduces the need for rework, thus saving time and resources. This leads to increased efficiency.

iii. **Enhanced reputation** - Organizations that consistently deliver high-quality work build a formidable reputation for excellence, which can attract new customers leading to more business and superior talent for delivering that business.

iv. **Increased employee morale** - Employees who take pride in their work and feel that they are contributing to a high-quality product or service tend to have higher job satisfaction and morale.

Quality serves as a silent ambassador for individuals, speaking volumes about their commitment.

How can you maintain quality at your workplace?

While Quality is a topic that has multiple books written on it, here are some practical aspects for maintaining quality in your work.

i.   **Requirement gathering** - Requirement gathering is a crucial aspect of ensuring quality in a project or product. It involves the process of gathering information and understanding the customer's needs and expectations. By conducting thorough requirement gathering, the project team can ensure that they have a clear understanding of what the customer wants, which can help to avoid misunderstandings and reduce the risk of errors and omissions.

Effective requirement gathering can also help to identify potential issues and roadblocks early in the project lifecycle, which can be addressed before they become major problems. This can help to reduce the cost and time required for rework, and ultimately lead to a higher quality outcome.

In addition, requirement gathering can also help to establish a clear scope and set expectations for the project, which can help prevent scope creep and ensure that the project is delivered on time and within budget.

In case of repeat or recurring request, you know that your customers' requirements will be similar, if not same. In such a case, you can create a requirement gathering checklist that can also be used for similar projects for other customers. You can also use this list to ask questions to your customers during the requirement gathering phase and elicit an explicit response from them on the requirements.

A best practice is to capture the requirement discussions with your stakeholders on email so that nothing is left open for interpretation at a later stage. If there is any ambiguity, clarify by asking questions until you are clear on what exactly the customer's problem or requirement is. You may want to share some sample outputs or templates with the customers to ensure that they have clarity on what they will get as an output or deliverable. If you doubt the feasibility of fulfilling a requirement, check with your colleagues or manager before committing to the customer.

ii. **Expectation setting** - The challenge with defining "good quality" is that it is subjective. What may be "excellent" quality for one customer may be just "good enough" for another. Make sure that you have a clear understanding of what is expected of you in terms of quality from your customer. This can include setting quality standards, defining success metrics, and creating a checklist of tasks to ensure everything is done to the expected level of quality.

iii. **Process excellence** - Following a process is a crucial part of ensuring superior quality work in the workplace. Many organizations have Standard Operating Procedures (SOPs) for processes. They provide a standardized, documented approach to carrying out specific tasks or processes, ensuring consistency and accuracy in execution. SOPs also act as a reference guide for employees to follow, reducing the risk of errors or deviations from established processes. Ensure you follow the SOP and also update them, as necessary.

When a process is followed, it also helps to identify potential problems early on, which can be addressed before they become bigger issues. Additionally, a process can help to identify areas for improvement and optimization, which can lead to increased efficiency and better-quality work in the long term. In order to ensure good quality work through following a process, it is important that you understand the process well, and why each step of the process is necessary. If needed, ask questions to clarify and gain a better understanding of the process.

Also, prepare a quality checklist (a list of checks to ensure that the final output is error free and meets customer expectations) if one is not existing already, and adhere to it diligently. You may even want to discuss with your customer on the quality checklist that you have prepared and seek their inputs to ensure its comprehensiveness. This can give a confidence boost to your customer because they will know that you have a strong quality process in place for your deliveries.

iv. **Automation** - Automation has become a popular approach to ensure quality in the workplace. Using technologies, you can automate the testing and inspection of products or services, reducing the likelihood of human error and inconsistency.

For example, in manufacturing, automated systems can inspect and test products as they move down the production line, detecting any defects or issues that might compromise quality. Similarly, in software development, automated testing tools can quickly and accurately identify bugs and errors in code, enabling developers to fix them before they impact users.

By automating quality control processes, businesses can improve their productivity, while also reducing costs associated with manual testing and inspection.

v. **Attention to detail** - Attention to detail refers to the ability to notice even the minutest details in a work process or outcome. By paying close attention to details, you can identify and correct any mistakes or errors, which in turn leads to a higher quality output.

Pay attention to details, as they can often make a substantial difference in the overall quality of the work. Double-checking your work, proofreading documents, and reviewing spreadsheets are all examples of ways to pay attention to details. This becomes critical for areas such as finance or employee compensation where accuracy is of paramount importance. In industries like manufacturing or construction, attention to detail can ensure that every part of the final product is assembled or built correctly, with no defects or errors.

If you are tasked with correcting one aspect of your work, go beyond addressing only the specified area. Take an extra step to thoroughly review your entire work, ensuring accuracy across all aspects. This proactive approach reduces the need for others to repeatedly revisit your work for corrections, emphasizing your commitment to delivering consistently high-quality results. Consider it your responsibility to create a high-quality output rather than someone else's responsibility to review your work and catch any errors.

In addition, attention to detail can also help you identify potential problems or issues before they become larger and costlier to fix. This not only helps maintain quality, but also saves time and resources. Therefore, by consistently demonstrating a strong attention to detail, you can contribute to a workplace culture that prioritizes quality and accuracy.

vi. **Formatting and aesthetics** - In the service industry, aesthetics and formatting play a crucial role in the delivery of services to clients. The visual appeal of a service delivery can significantly impact how it is perceived by clients. A well-formatted and aesthetically pleasing presentation can convey professionalism, attention to detail, and a commitment to quality, which are essential for building trust and confidence in the service provider.

However, some people may overlook the significance of aesthetics and formatting, instead focusing solely on delivering the core content of the deliverables. Neglecting the look and feel of the deliverable can have adverse effects on client sentiment. A poorly formatted or aesthetically unpleasing service delivery may fail to resonate with clients, even if the content itself is valuable.

Clients are not only interested in the substance of the service but also in its presentation as aesthetics and formatting not only enhance the visual appeal of a service delivery but also contribute to better clarity and understanding. Sometimes our immediate clients may have to present deliverables to their stakeholders in their own organization. In that case, it becomes paramount to pay attention to aesthetics and formatting for ensuring a positive client experience and maintaining strong client relationships.

vii. **Change management** - In my experience, issues are more likely to occur when changes happen. Below are a few types of changes that you would encounter in your projects:

a. *Change of people/team member* - When a team member transitions to a new role or resigns, it necessitates a shift in personnel for the project. This change may result in the loss of implicit knowledge from the departing team member. It is crucial to document as much tacit knowledge as possible and establish a robust transition plan between the two team members with clear timelines and a buffer period to accommodate any unforeseen delays.

b. *Change of customer point of contact* - If there is a change in the customer point of contact, incomplete transition at their end is likely. The new customer may be unfamiliar with their own internal processes, leading to the possibility of providing 'incorrect' or incomplete data. Therefore, be extra cautious when receiving inputs from new customers for the first time to spot any issues that may have crept in. Any changes in requirements or expectations due to change in customer should be captured and documented from the beginning and evaluated for any scope creep compared to the original project scope. It is a good practice to on-board the new customer by walking them through the required data, processes, project timelines, milestones, and deliverables. I have seen appreciations by customers for smooth onboarding by the service-provider as it helps them settle well into their new role.

c. *Change of requirements, rules,* or *process* - Changes in business rules or process necessitate a thorough assessment of their impact across your deliverables. It is important to diligently understand the new requirements and document them in collaboration with the customer. In a complex project with multiple deliverables, use a checklist to evaluate which deliverables will and will not be impacted by the change. Ensure that all the new requirements are incorporated before final delivery to customers using a checklist.

d. *Technology Changes* - Upgrades or changes in the technology stack may require adjustments to your processes and workflows. When migrating or updating technology, ensure that the existing processes do not get impacted. Adhere to your organization's process of software testing to minimize any issues.

e. *Vendor or Supplier Changes* - If your project involves external vendors or suppliers, changes in their services or partnerships can impact your project dynamics. Ensure you work with them to minimize impact on your project during such a change.

Note: After around 10 years into my corporate career, I understood the importance of many elements included in this book. When working with global teams or supporting other regions or countries, the quality of our work and how we approach it, also plays a role in shaping the image of our country. For instance, if we provide consistent, excellent work to the customer, they will perceive the people in our country to be diligent and highly professional. Conversely, if there are repeated issues with our work, it can create a perception that people in our country are casual and unprofessional. Therefore, it is crucial to remember that when supporting your customers in a global setting, you are not just representing your organization but also your country, and how you conduct yourself and deliver your work will shape the perception of your country. In my view, this is a significant responsibility and an opportunity to build a positive image not just for yourself or your organization, but also for your country.

SUMMARY

In conclusion, this chapter underscores the critical role of quality in shaping customer experiences, organizational success, and even national reputations. Through relatable scenarios like pizza deliveries, the importance of meeting customer expectations becomes apparent.

The advantages of maintaining quality in products and services are manifold, ranging from better customer satisfaction and improved efficiency to enhanced reputation and increased employee morale. Quality not only speaks volumes about an organization's commitment but also serves as a silent ambassador for you.

Self-Reflection

i.   *What best practices do I follow to ensure quality in my work?*

ii. *What more can I do to maintain or further improve quality of my work?*

5.

THE ART OF TIMELINESS

Mastering the art of timeliness is not only a testament to professionalism but also a catalyst for productivity and success. Meeting timelines or deadlines refers to the ability to deliver work on time, honor commitments, and ensuring that the agreed-upon schedules are adhered to. Meeting deadlines is a crucial aspect of professional conduct.

Timeliness is not just about being on time for meetings or submitting reports on time, but it is also about being proactive and anticipating deadlines in advance. In a fast-paced work environment, it is essential to prioritize timeliness to meet the demands of the industry and ensure that work is completed efficiently.

Let us go back to the pizza scenario in the previous chapter. Imagine that you get the pizza with the same toppings you had ordered, but perhaps an hour later compared to the expected delivery time - how would you feel? Most likely disappointed or frustrated, especially if you were hungry and had been eagerly waiting for the pizza. Our customers will have similar experience if they do not receive their product or service as per the scheduled or committed timelines.

Meeting deadlines is not just a work ethic; it's a promise to excellence, a testament to reliability, and a key to professional success.

Benefits of meeting deadlines at workplace

Consistently delivering your work on time has many advantages:

i.   **Creates a good first impression** - Being on time is one of the simplest ways to create a good impression on your stakeholders.

ii. **Builds trust** - Being punctual for meetings, deadlines, and deliverables is crucial in building a good reputation and gaining the trust of colleagues and managers. It also demonstrates a commitment to the job and a willingness to go the extra mile to ensure that tasks are completed on time.

iii. **Bolsters your personal brand** - Being timely shows that the employee is dependable, responsible, and respects the time of their colleagues and customers. An employee who consistently delivers their work on time will stand out and be recognized as a valuable asset to the organization.

iv. **Reduces stress** - Meeting deadlines can be stressful, but timely completion of tasks reduces the pressure of last-minute rush, leading to a more peaceful work environment.

How can you exhibit timeliness?

i.   **Create a plan** - Create a plan that outlines the specific tasks that need to be completed within a particular timeframe. This can help you prioritize your work and ensure that you are on track to meet the deadlines. Share this plan with your stakeholders, as needed, to be aligned with them on timelines.

ii. **Meet deadlines** - As an employee, it is important to establish yourself as a trusted professional. One way to do this is by completing tasks and projects on time. For example, if your manager assigns you a task with a deadline, make sure you complete it on or before the deadline. This shows that you are reliable and can be trusted to deliver work on time. On the other hand, if you consistently miss deadlines, it can create a negative impression and affect your career growth.

iii. **Be punctual** - Being punctual is another important aspect of timeliness. Arriving on time for work, meetings, and training sessions shows that you are respectful of other people's time and value the importance of being present when required. It also shows that you are organized and can manage your time effectively. Being consistently late can have a negative impact on your reputation and can affect your ability to build relationships with colleagues and supervisors.

iv. **Be organized** - Being organized can help you manage your time efficiently. Ensure that your work area is clean, and your documents are arranged in an orderly manner. Use tools such as calendars, reminders, and to-do lists to stay on top of your tasks and deadlines.

v. **Use time-management techniques** - Use techniques such as prioritization and delegation to manage your time efficiently. Prioritizing helps you focus on the most important tasks, while delegation allows you to distribute the workload effectively. You may not be able to delegate your work in the initial stages of your career when you are in individual contributor. However, this becomes an important aspect as you get into a leadership role.

What if you are unable to meet deadlines? It is essential to communicate any potential risks to meeting deadlines to your manager as early as possible. When highlighting such issues, it is important to share not just the problem, but also the reason the task cannot be completed on time and what support will potentially help you complete the task closest to the deadline. By doing this, you can help your manager provide you necessary support to ensure timely completion of the task.

Generally, timely completion of customer deliverables will be a higher priority compared to internal tasks, except when it is related to important internal meetings with a fixed date such as a monthly or quarterly business review. Regardless of the nature of the task, it is important to have a clear understanding of it, seek clarification if needed, and strive to complete all tasks within the given timeline.

It is important to note that if delays happen repeatedly, it may be necessary to identify the underlying issue and discuss with your manager to find a sustainable solution to avoid negative impact on your performance.

What if you are unable to attend a meeting or training on time? If you have accepted an invitation to a meeting or training, and you are unable to join on time, it is important to inform the organizer as early as possible. It is best to provide a reason for your delay, and if you can inform them in advance, which is even better. This shows that you respect the time of others and take your commitments seriously.

Note: If you are collaborating with people in different time zones, when agreeing or committing to timelines, be sure to specify which time zone you are referring to in order to avoid unnecessary confusion. For example, if you are working with a US customer, simply saying that you will send a deliverable to them by 'end of the day' will not suffice. Specify if it is your end of the day or your customer's end of the day.

SUMMARY

Mastering the art of timeliness is not just a professional virtue but a strategic advantage. From meeting deadlines to seizing opportunities with precision timing, the ability to prioritize timeliness is a hallmark of professionalism and a driver of productivity and success.

Meeting deadlines is not merely about delivering work on time; it is also about honouring your commitments. Consistently meeting deadlines requires careful planning, organization, and effective time-management techniques. However, if deadlines cannot be met, proactive communication with stakeholders is crucial. Mastering the art of timeliness fosters a culture of reliability, accountability, and professionalism that contributes to your as well as organizational success.

Self-Reflection

i.   *How do I ensure keeping time commitments with my stakeholders?*

ii. *What can I do more to maintain or further improve timeliness of my work?*

6.

THRIVING WITH OWNERSHIP AND ACCOUNTABILITY

Taking ownership and accountability at workplace means being responsible and accountable for one's actions and decisions, as well as their consequences. It means finding solutions to problems, rather than simply shifting blame to someone else or to external factors. It also means being committed to achieving goals, meeting deadlines, and taking responsibility of the outcome of projects or tasks. This requires a sense of initiative, a willingness to take risks and accept feedback, and learning from mistakes. Taking ownership and accountability are important traits for building trust and credibility with colleagues, customers, and other stakeholders, and is a key factor in career success. Still, it is common to find people who completely disregard this aspect at work.

If a manager can discover and hire talent with high ownership and accountability, their job is half done. Such employees will accomplish tasks assigned to them within specified deadlines. If the task is expected to take longer, they keep their manager informed about the progress without follow-ups. This provides the manager a profound sense of relief as they can be assured that the work is on track, will be completed on time and they will be updated of any risks encountered on the way. It also fosters trust between the manager and direct report which in turn leads to more delegation by the manager to the employee resulting in growth and advancement for the employee.

Individuals who demonstrate a sense of ownership and accountability take full responsibility of their tasks. They adhere to established procedures and standards to maintain quality and compliance, without taking any shortcuts. If an error is detected, they take responsibility for it, express genuine regret, and take necessary steps to rectify the situation. As this behavior becomes consistent over time, the manager starts building trust in these individuals and becomes increasingly dependent on them. Such individuals are highly valued by managers and sought after.

Mastering ownership and accountability is the subtle key to unlocking career advancement and personal growth.

The ownership and accountability for these associates does not just end with projects. They understand that they are responsible for their own growth and development. They create their own development plan in alignment with their manager and follow through on the actions required to actualize the plan. They take feedback seriously and work on it.

To contrast, there are individuals who do not initiate their work in a timely manner nor provide progress updates to the manager. This leads the manager to constantly follow-up with them to ensure that they stay on track and complete the task. The manager must keep the task at the top of their own priorities to prevent missing any deadlines. These individuals display a lack of accountability and ownership towards their work. They often present reasons for why tasks were not accomplished or why their work contained errors. They may also opt for shortcuts, disregarding the process to be followed. As a result, they lose the manager's confidence and opportunities for growth and development. These individuals also tend to exhibit dissatisfaction when their performance evaluation or promotion outcomes do not align with their expectations. They may also complain of their manager 'micromanaging' them.

Example

An example of exhibiting ownership and accountability could be when an employee takes the initiative to resolve an issue without being prompted by their manager or team leader. For instance, if a customer raises a concern about a product or service, an employee who takes ownership and accountability would proactively work towards addressing the issue and providing a solution to the customer. This could involve coordinating with different teams, conducting a deep dive analysis, and providing regular updates to the customer. By taking ownership of the issue, the employee not only ensures customer satisfaction but also demonstrates their commitment to the success of the organization.

On the other hand, there are people who will provide delayed delivery or send bad-quality work to the customer without much botheration. They do not really care of what the customer thinks or feels of their sub-standard work or how it reflects on their organization. For them, they just had to deliver, and they did.

Which category of employees would you want to be in - one that the manager can trust with opportunities or the one that the manager would avoid taking bets on?

What are the advantages of taking ownership and accountability?

i. **Builds trust** - When you take ownership of your work and are accountable for your actions, it can build trust among your colleagues and superiors. People will see that you are reliable and responsible, which can enhance your professional reputation.

ii. **Increases productivity** - Taking ownership and accountability can lead to increased productivity, as you are focused on completing tasks to the best of your abilities.

This can also result in better time management and task prioritization.

iii. **Facilitates personal growth** - When you take ownership and accountability consistently, you develop a healthy habit. You are more likely to seek out as well as attract opportunities for personal and professional growth. This can help you to develop new skills, take on new challenges, and advance in your career.

iv. **Greater job satisfaction**: When you take ownership of your work, you are more likely to feel a sense of accomplishment and satisfaction, which can lead to greater job satisfaction and success.

How can you take ownership and accountability at workplace?

i. **Respect organization's trust** - By being customer-oriented, you can demonstrate respect for the trust that the organization has placed in you. The organization has hired you for the role with the expectation that you will do your job well and thereby provide its customers a positive experience. Take this opportunity to acknowledge the organization's trust in you and commit to fulfilling their expectations to the best of your ability.

ii. **Pause and reflect** - Take a moment to step back and observe the effects of your work on your customers, as it can be easy to become so engrossed in your tasks that you lose sight of the bigger picture. A realization of how your work impacts your customers will prompt you to go a step forward in taking ownership and accountability. Talk to your manager if you need help in understanding how your work contributes to the bigger picture.

iii. **Have a sense of gratitude** - The organization provides compensation for your efforts, and this enables you and your family to lead a comfortable life. Therefore, it is important to feel appreciative toward both the organization and its customers for entrusting you with the opportunity to sustain yourself and your loved ones. Express this gratitude by delivering the highest level of service to ensure customer satisfaction.

Taking Ownership and Accountability means "taking care" of:

* Projects
* Team members, and
* Customers

on one's own without being told or reminded to do so. Below is a list of activities (comprehensive but not exhaustive) that you can consider for taking ownership and accountability at work for a data analysis project. This could be a good starting point for you to take ownership and accountability and can be tweaked based on your team's requirement.

Before the project

i.   Initiate discussions with customers/stakeholders

ii. Prepare project plan - keep customer updated on the plan.

iii. Prepare and share data formats/template.

iv. Follow-up during data collection stage, as required.

v.   Check with customer on timelines to receive the data.

vi. Perform data validation checks on receiving the data - highlight missing data, outliers, anomalies and ask clarifying question.

vii. In case of data issues, ask for updated/correct data.

viii. Send minutes of meetings

ix. Revisit timelines in case of data issues.

Note: Is sending incorrect data customer's problem? Or an opportunity for you to highlight data issues, build customer trust, and establish yourself as a diligent professional?

During the project

i. Begin the analysis.

ii. Keep the customer updated of the progress, perhaps weekly, even if the project is on track, to be transparent and give them a reassurance that they are in safe hands.

iii. Follow process documents (standard operating procedures (SOPs) and quality (QC) checklists)

iv. Keep the project manager updated of any potential risks, issues, and delays.

v. Get your work validated by a peer before sharing with customer, if needed

vi. Deliver preliminary analysis to the customer.

vii. Schedule meeting with customer much in advance (rather than the same day or a day before, unless unavoidable) to discuss the analysis and get their initial reaction/feedback.

viii. If something is incorrect or customer gives constructive feedback or suggestions, be open to them.

ix. Be on time for meetings.

x. Take notes and share them with meeting attendees within a day, with discussion points and action items.

xi. Track and complete action items from meetings.

xii. Incorporate feedback into the analysis.

xiii. Prepare final analysis.

xiv. Share final analysis with customer for their use for decision making.

xv. Work on shared location or update documents regularly on shared location.

After the project

i.   If there is no acknowledgment from the customer, follow-up to check with them on the analysis.

ii. Create project closure document with learnings.

iii. Place all pending documents in a shared location for future reference.

iv. Prepare case study for capability presentations for future proposals.

The signs to watch-out for which display lack of ownership and accountability:

i.   'Switch-off' after 'kick-off' - no follow-ups with customer after the kick-off meeting.

ii. No project plan in place and no periodic updates to customer on project status.

iii. No minutes of meeting after telephonic/video calls.

iv. Hiding an issue or customer bringing-up an issue.

v.   Lack of quality - because a peer will anyway review before sharing with customer.

vi. Consistently scheduling meetings at the last minute.

vii. Not updating documents on shared location.

SUMMARY

Remember that owning your actions and being accountable is not just a job requirement - it is a pathway to personal and professional growth. When you take ownership and accountability, you demonstrate reliability, commitment, and a proactive approach to problem-solving. Your managers truly value employees like you, as they can trust you with responsibilities and opportunities for advancement.

But it is not limited to tasks alone. Embracing ownership and accountability means taking charge of your personal development and fostering trust with colleagues and clients. By consistently embodying these qualities, you not only become an indispensable asset to your organization but also pave the way for your own success and growth. Reflect on the advantages, and actively implement strategies to foster a culture of ownership and accountability within yourself and your team.

Self-Reflection

i. *How can I integrate ownership and accountability into my daily work routines and interactions with colleagues?*

ii. *What areas of my work could benefit from a deeper sense of ownership and accountability, and what steps can I take to improve in those areas?*

7.

MASTERING PROCESS ORIENTATION

Being process-oriented in an organization means focusing on the methods, procedures, and systems used to accomplish tasks and achieve goals, rather than solely on delivering the end results. This means that if there is a task to be completed, it needs to be completed in a certain way, irrespective of who does it. Processes are an important determinant of organizational effectiveness. The extent to which you will need to comply with the process may vary depending on the industry you operate in.

Adherence to processes is the unseen force behind organizational excellence where each action is a step towards efficiency, reliability, and success.

Example

Consider this example that highlights the significance of strict process adherence. My team played a crucial role in supporting a customer with a project involving financial payment calculation for its employees. Unfortunately, a payment calculation error occurred, leading to incorrect amount being paid to several employees. Upon investigation, it became evident that the mistake was not attributable to our team's oversight. The team had meticulously adhered to the process by engaging in detailed discussions with the customer about business rules, creating sample calculations, and rigorously following a comprehensive quality checklist. The root cause of the error was in the interpretation of the documented business rules, which led to a disparity in how payments were calculated by the team compared to the customer's expectations. Despite the customer's dissatisfaction, our adept handling of the situation was possible due to the unwavering adherence to the process without any gaps. Had there been any lapses in process, we would have found ourselves in a potentially embarrassing situation.

Rigorously following the process not only prevented internal finger-pointing or blame games regarding the situation, but also ensured that accountability was attributed to the process rather than to any individual team member. This allowed the team to concentrate on improving the process, ensuring precise definition of business rules, and eliminating any room for ambiguity or misinterpretation in the future.

How does it help to be process oriented?

i. **Consistency** - Following a set of defined processes ensures that work is done consistently, regardless of who is doing it. This consistency can improve the quality of work and help avoid errors or mistakes.

ii. **Efficiency** - Processes are designed to be efficient and reduce waste. By following a set process, employees can work more quickly and with fewer errors, which can save time and resources. Processes also help new employees to come to speed faster.

iii. **Scalability** - As a company grows, it becomes increasingly important to have a set of processes in place that can be scaled up to handle larger volumes of work. By being process oriented, a company can ensure that it can continue to deliver high-quality work even as it grows.

iv. **Compliance** - Many industries have regulations or standards that companies must comply with. By having defined processes in place, companies can ensure that they are meeting these requirements and avoiding legal or financial penalties.

v. **Continuous improvement** - By following a set process, companies can more easily identify areas for improvement and make changes to improve efficiency, quality, or compliance. This continuous improvement can help a company stay competitive and adapt to changing market conditions.

How can you demonstrate process orientation in your work?

i. **Automate processes** – Wherever possible, automate processes using technology. This will ensure that the required steps are followed consistently and variation due to human intervention are eliminated.

ii. **Create, follow, and update SOPs** - Standard Operating Procedures (SOPs) are step-by-step instructions for completing a specific task or process. They are designed to ensure consistency, quality, and efficiency in the work being done. To demonstrate process orientation, for steps that cannot be fully automated, you should create SOPs for your work processes if they don't already exist, follow them consistently, and regularly update them to reflect any changes or improvements in the process. This helps to ensure that work is completed in a standardized and efficient manner. You can also share this as a best practice in your team or function.

iii. **Create, follow, and update quality checklists** - Quality checklists are tools used to ensure that work meets specific quality standards or criteria. To demonstrate process orientation, you should create quality checklists for your project tasks, follow them consistently, and regularly update them to reflect any changes or improvements in the quality standards or criteria. If there is any mistake in the deliverable, you should follow the process defined in your organization, which should typically include updating the QC checklist, creating an RCA (root cause analysis), and completing the corrective and preventive actions. This helps to ensure that work meets the required quality standards and reduces the likelihood of errors or defects.

iv. **Maintain document version control** - Document version control is the process of managing different versions of a document to ensure that the most current and accurate version is being used. To demonstrate process orientation, you should maintain document version control by clearly labeling documents with version numbers or dates, saving them in a central location where they can be easily accessed and updated, and ensuring that all team members are using the most current version of the document. This helps to ensure that everyone is working from the same information and reduces the risk of errors or miscommunication due to outdated information. For example, for a monthly deliverable for July 2024, you can name a file as *202407_Filename_v1.0* and as you make subsequent changes, you can create another version and name the file as *202407_Filename_v1.1* for minor changes or *202407_Filename_v2.0* for major changes. You should consider the file nomenclature being followed in your team to be consistent.

Note: While sticking to processes helps in many ways, you need to be intelligent enough to understand when you need to deviate from the process, especially when these deviations are not a part of the process, to provide a great customer experience. Deviation from the process may be required due to unforeseen circumstances, changes in the project requirements, or if the process itself is not producing the desired results. However, it is important to note that any deviation from the process should be aligned or approved by relevant stakeholders, such as your manager or customer. Additionally, it is essential to document the reasons for the deviation and its potential impact on the project. In general, it is important to strive for a balance between process adherence and flexibility to adapt to changing circumstances and deliver the best customer experience.

SUMMARY

In summary, mastering process orientation is vital for organizational excellence. Consistency, efficiency, scalability, compliance, and continuous improvement are just a few of the benefits that come from being process oriented.

To demonstrate process orientation in your work, creating, following, and updating SOPs, quality checklists, and maintaining document version control are crucial steps. However, it is also important to recognize when deviations from the process are necessary, especially to provide exceptional customer experiences. Any deviations should be aligned with stakeholders and documented appropriately as much as possible. Striking a balance between adherence to processes and flexibility is key to navigating changing circumstances and delivering outstanding results.

Self-Reflection

i.   *Do I feel appreciated for consistently adhering to processes? If not, how do I keep myself going?*

ii. *How consistently do I follow established processes in my work, and how has this impacted the quality and efficiency of my output?*

8.

BEING PROACTIVE

Being proactive in the workplace involves taking initiative and pre-emptively addressing issues rather than waiting for them to arise and reacting afterwards. It involves identifying opportunities for improvement, taking action to address potential issues, and being accountable for the outcomes of one's actions. Proactive individuals are self-motivated and take responsibility for their own work and the success of their team, rather than relying on others to guide them. They tend to be more effective and successful in their roles and can contribute to a positive and productive work environment.

Do not wait for opportunities; create them. Proactivity is the key that unlocks doors to success.

Being reactive, on the other hand, involves responding to a problem or situation after it has occurred. This often means that the response is driven by the urgency of the situation rather than a planned approach. While reactivity is required and can be important in certain situations, it is often less effective than being proactive as it can lead to a cycle of constantly reacting to problems rather than preventing them in the first place.

Going back to the pizza scenarios that we discussed in chapter four on 'Pursuing Quality Excellence': If the company were proactive and communicated to you of the anticipated delay in pizza delivery with a reasonable explanation for the delay, you perhaps would be more at ease. And on top of it, if they offered a compensation like a discount coupon or made the delivery free, they most likely converted a dissatisfied customer into a happy one. This is the power of being proactive and taking steps to ensure positive customer experience remains a top priority for the organization.

Example

Imagine a situation where you are supporting a customer on a project. Your customer's supervisor writes to your manager informing them of project delay because of you. On enquiring with you, your manager learns that there was an instance of one-week delay from your side due to medical emergency. However, you know that there were also instances where inputs and feedback were pending from your customer, which caused project timelines to extend beyond the planned schedule. The manager asks you the following questions:

i.   Was a project plan created which had the original milestones and planned timelines?

ii. Was the delay from your side communicated to the customer when it occurred?

iii. Was the customer informed that your medical emergency would impact overall project timelines?

iv. Was the customer informed that the delay in their inputs and feedback will impact overall project timelines?

If your manager was not already aware of the situation, they might ask why you did not inform them proactively. Being proactive in this case meant that you communicated with your manager about the situations as they happened, anticipated how the customer would respond to those situations and managed their expectations accordingly. This also had to be flagged as a risk internally to avoid any surprize escalations. Given the situation now, your manager suggests a way forward as follows:

i.   Avoid getting into the blame game on whether you or your customer caused the delay. It will not help move things forward.

ii. Acknowledge the delay from your side and also indicate, in a subtle manner, that inputs and feedback from customer also impacted the plan.

iii. Look forward and show commitment to complete the project at the earliest.

iv. Create a plan for the upcoming activities with milestones, highlight dependencies and provide a timeline by when the project can be completed. Call out assumptions made e.g., that the data will arrive on time.

v.   Highlight learnings from the situation and how you would do things differently in future in similar situations.

How does it help to be proactive at workplace?

i.   **Increased productivity** - Proactive employees are always looking for ways to improve their work processes, identify potential problems before they arise, and take initiative to address issues. This helps them to work more efficiently and effectively, ultimately leading to increased productivity.

ii. **Career advancement** - Proactive employees are often seen as valuable assets to the organization, and their initiative and problem-solving skills can lead to career advancement opportunities. They may be given more responsibilities, promoted to higher positions, or considered for special projects or initiatives.

iii. **Improved job satisfaction** - Proactive employees are more engaged and invested in their work, which can lead to greater job satisfaction. By taking ownership of their work and contributing to the success of the team or organization, they feel a sense of pride and accomplishment.

iv. **Better relationships with colleagues** - Proactive employees are more likely to collaborate with others, seek feedback, and share knowledge and expertise. This can lead to stronger relationships with colleagues, a more positive work environment, and better overall outcomes for the team or organization.

v. **Improved personal development** - By taking initiative and seeking out new challenges and opportunities, proactive employees are constantly learning and developing new skills. This can benefit both you as well as the organization.

Below are a few examples of being proactive at the workplace:

i. **Highlight spare capacity** - If you have idle time, highlight it to your manager and offer help. This shows that you have an open mind, you are not shy of contributing more, learning new things, and working hard.

ii. **Share periodic updates** - If you are assigned a task that needs to be complete in a longer duration, say a month, keep your stakeholder updated weekly on where you are and that you are on track. Idea is to avoid any follow-ups from stakeholders on the status and responding reactively to their queries.

iii. **Flag delays** - If you anticipate a delay in completing the assigned task, convey to your manager on the delay as soon as possible with the reason and seek his advice on how to keep it on track. If it impacts the client, work with your manager to communicate it to them. Ideally, if you have built a good relationship with your client, you should be in a position to communicate this to them by yourself.

iv. **Nominate yourself for initiatives** - In a team meeting, if your manager is asking for a nomination for something, raise your hand to take that task. It shows that you are willing to support on things that matter.

v. **Share your thoughts** - If you observe that something is not working well in the team or something can be done in a better way, discuss with your manager and propose improvement ideas. If your manager is aligned, you can also implement those ideas in your team.

vi. **Plan your leaves** - If you are planning to be on leave, inform your manager, team, and customer in advance, identify a back-up, and plan your work accordingly.

vii. **Prioritize activities** - If you need to prioritize your tasks, ensure that you are coordinated with your manager, especially if it is related to customer deliveries or product schedule.

The table below gives you some practical examples of the difference between a reactive approach and a proactive approach of handling situations:

Reactive Approach	Proactive Approach
After you do the analysis, you figure out at the end that the data shared by the customer was incorrect.	Doing the data check/validation first and highlighting any potential issues to the customer upfront before beginning the analysis.
Make assumptions on your own, perform the analysis and share with your customer.	Discuss the relevance of your assumptions with your customer before performing the analysis and tweaking them as required.

Customer discusses a request today. They send the data three weeks later. You do not follow-up with the customer.	Follow-up with the customer within a week for status of data for the discussed request.
In a report, 4 out of 6 reports are ready to be delivered, while data for 2 reports is pending from the customer. You plan to deliver all 6 reports in a single go.	You give options to the customer - if they would prefer to get the 4 completed reports now, and the 2 later once you have the data for them; or if they would prefer to have all 6 reports together in a single go. You deliver the reports as the client prefers.
A team member shared a request for some data, and you do not share the data by the requested timeline. They have to follow-up with you.	You share the data with your team member without them having to follow-up with you. Or in case of an anticipated delay from your side, you inform your team member about the potential delay and check if it will be okay for them.
You plan to be on leave the following week and inform your stakeholders on the last day before going on vacation.	You plan and inform your stakeholders about your absence 2 to 3 weeks in advance and also let them know of your back-up while you will be away.

SUMMARY

Being proactive in the workplace is essential for ensuring positive outcomes and maintaining a high standard of performance. By taking initiatives, addressing issues before they escalate, and communicating effectively, you can contribute to increased productivity, career advancement, job satisfaction, better relationships with colleagues, and personal development. Contrasting reactive and proactive approaches illustrates the significant impact of proactive behavior in various situations, emphasizing the importance of proactive action in fostering success and positive outcomes in the workplace.

Self-Reflection

i.   *How often do I anticipate potential issues or challenges in my work and take proactive steps to address them before they become problems?*

ii. *How do I ensure that people do not have to follow-up with me on a request?*

9.

GOING THE EXTRA MILE

Going the extra mile at the workplace means putting in extra effort beyond what is expected to achieve a desired outcome or **to provide exceptional experience** to colleagues or customers. It involves taking initiative, going beyond the minimum requirements, and demonstrating a willingness to contribute to the success of the team or organization.

While going **the** extra mile does not guarantee rewards, it often increases the likelihood of recognition and career growth. It demonstrates a strong work ethic, dedication, and commitment to achieving exceptional results, which is highly valued by most employers. In addition, going **beyond** the call of duty can help build a positive reputation, enhance job satisfaction, and create a sense of pride and accomplishment in one's work.

In the journey of success, going the extra mile is the path where dedication turns ordinary efforts into extraordinary achievements.

Example

One of my team members had been working on a project for two years and wanted a change. We agreed to move her to a new project in the coming quarter. Although the transition period had not yet arrived, she began acquiring the necessary skills for the new project and started gradually transferring her current responsibilities to another team member. While she was able to learn the new skills, transition for her current projects was lagging due to new team member's slow adaptation. However, she ensured that the project delivery for her new as well as current project went smooth. That entailed working long hours on weekdays and working over a few weekends. She had gone the extra mile to ensure that customer experience does not get adversely impacted on her current projects because of incomplete or inadequate transition to the next team member taking up that project.

What are the benefits of going the extra mile at workplace?

i.   **Builds a positive reputation** - By consistently going above and beyond what is expected of you, you can build a positive reputation as a dedicated and reliable employee.

ii. **Career advancement** - Your willingness to take on additional responsibilities and exceed expectations can make you stand out to your superiors and increase your chances of career advancement.

iii. **Personal growth and development** - Pushing yourself to go the extra mile can also help you develop new skills, gain new experiences, and broaden your knowledge base.

iv. **Increased job satisfaction** - When you take pride in your work and strive to do your best, you can experience a greater sense of fulfilment and satisfaction in your job.

v.   **Improved relationships** - Going the extra mile can also help you build better relationships with your colleagues and superiors, as they are more likely to appreciate and respect your efforts.

How can you go the extra mile at workplace?

i.   **Be willing to help** - Imagine two team members working on a project when one of them has a personal emergency and takes urgent leave. This puts the project timeline at risk. The manager is looking for someone to help complete the project on time. You can step in to support the project and ensure it is delivered on schedule.

ii. **Open to stretch for learning** - A new customer has signed up for a three-month project. This new opportunity can significantly benefit the organization's growth. All current team members are occupied with ongoing projects. You can volunteer for this project for even though you are nearly fully occupied with other tasks as this is only a short-term project. This will enhance your learning and contribute to the organization's growth.

iii. **Customer orientation** - A customer needs a deliverable sooner than the planned timeline, requiring you to work over the weekend to meet the new deadline. You should inquire about the reason for urgency, which might be, for example, due to an upcoming senior leadership visit at customer end. If feasible, you can work over the weekend to deliver the project. Additionally, ask the customer if they need further support for the leadership visit. Align with your manager, as it might involve extra work beyond the original project scope. This approach can help build a trusted relationship with the customer, going beyond the immediate work.

iv. **Learning** - If your team has a unique project requiring skills no one currently possesses, you can take the opportunity to research, learn, and successfully deliver the project.

v. **Cross-team or cross-functional collaboration** - You can offer your skill set to assist other teams based on their needs. This is especially valuable when those teams face challenges such as a high number of issues, staff unavailability, or a new project with limited resources. Your support will be appreciated during these times. After completing the project, you can share the best practices from the other team with your own team. You will also get a view of the work done in the other team and it could be the next thing you would like to pursue in your career.

Note: While it helps to go the extra mile to support the team or organization, it is crucial to uphold a balanced work-life equilibrium and avoid compromising personal well-being for professional accomplishments. Therefore, only extend your efforts at work to the extent that it facilitates learning and development and aids the team or organization in achieving their goals without negatively affecting your health and personal relationships. Occasional stretching to address genuine business needs with a clear endpoint is acceptable and appreciated. However, if it becomes a recurring pattern, it may be necessary to discuss the matter with your manager. Do a fair and honest assessment of your workload and your capacity to manage stretch engagements and nominate yourself for those opportunities accordingly.

SUMMARY

It is evident that the pathway to career success is paved with dedication, initiative, and a willingness to exceed expectations. Going beyond the call of duty is not merely a commendable gesture; it is a fundamental approach that distinguishes exceptional professionals from the rest. By consistently demonstrating a commitment to excellence, you not only enhance your reputation but also foster personal growth and satisfaction. However, it is important to strike a balance between professional ambition and personal well-being, ensuring that efforts align with sustainable growth and fulfilment. Hence, do a fair assessment of your current workload and ability to stretch, and nominate for going the extra mile accordingly.

Self-Reflection

i.   *When was the last time I had to learn something on the go to deliver on a project?*

ii.   *If I were to ask my customers how I have helped them in urgent situations, what would their likely response be?*

10.

ELEVATING CUSTOMER EXPERIENCE

Customer orientation or customer centricity is about focusing on the needs and preferences of customers in order to provide them with the best possible products or services. It involves understanding and anticipating the needs and expectations of customers, aligning business processes and strategies to meet those needs, listening to customer feedback, and continuously improving products or services based on that feedback. Customer orientation is about putting the customer at the centre of everything a business does. For any organization, its customers are the reason for its very existence, and hence they should never be taken for granted, unless of course, the plan is to shut down the business!

At workplace, there is a broad spectrum of customer orientation exhibited by individuals. On one end, there are people who demonstrate a strong commitment to customer satisfaction and deploy many of the best practices described in this book to ensure customers get the best possible experience from them and their organization. On the other hand, I have observed others who show little regard for customer experience. They do not acknowledge inquiries from customers, and it takes follow-ups from customers before a response is provided. Their approach to work is lackadaisical, which often leads to issues escalating. In such situations, the employee's manager or even higher-level management may need to become involved to address the situation and prevent customer loss.

It should be easy for anyone to imagine the anticipated customer feedback for these two ways of supporting customers and the impact on performance of these two categories of people.

To deliver outstanding service to your customers, prioritize assisting them in making a meaningful contribution toward their organizational goals. When a customer engages your services, it is your responsibility to fulfil your commitments. Your customer operates within a larger organizational context at their end. Thus, ensure your work not only aligns with their objectives but also helps them create positive outcomes within their organization. This can lead to recognition and appreciation for your customer, which in turn may benefit you. Satisfied customers are more likely to advocate for your products and services, resulting in increased business for your organization.

To put it plainly, you can envision the sequence of events like this for a business to business (B2B) situation:

i.   You provide the customer with your product or service.

ii. This has a positive impact on the customer's organization, for instance, higher sales for them.

iii. As a result, the customer shares appreciation with you and may even provide additional business to your organization.

Even for business-to-consumer (B2C) or direct-to-consumer (D2C) brands, it is imperative that they provide great products and services to their customers, which will help them get repeat and referral business.

It is crucial to acknowledge that from the customer's perspective, it is the organization that delivers the product or service, regardless of the individual they interact with.

Career success begins with customer orientation - where understanding needs turns into exceptional service, creating a path to endless opportunities.

Example

On one occasion, a team member made a mistake on a project, and I addressed the issue with the customer, providing a root cause analysis and outlining our action plan to prevent its recurrence. However, in the subsequent quarter, a different team member assumed responsibility for the same project with the same customer. Despite a smooth transition, a new issue arose during the new team member's initial delivery.

From each individual employee's standpoint, they made the mistake only once. However, for the customer, it constituted consecutive mistakes in successive quarters. They would not differentiate who made the mistake because they are accountable for results to their stakeholders. Handling that situation was challenging, but I implemented additional measures to ensure zero chance of error for the next few quarters on the same project. For instance, a second highly performing, more experienced individual would thoroughly review the work before delivering it to the customer starting from the subsequent quarter. This approach allowed us to enhance quality once again and rebuild the customer's trust.

The key point I want to emphasize is to consider situations from the customer's perspective rather than solely from your own or your company's viewpoint. Ultimately, you've joined the organization to serve and support customers. As mentioned earlier, that is the raison d'être for any organization.

What are the advantages of being customer oriented?

i.   **Increased customer satisfaction and retention** - By understanding customer needs and preferences, you can deliver products or services that meet their expectations, resulting in higher customer satisfaction. When customers are satisfied with your products or services, they are more likely to stay loyal to your brand and continue to do business with you.

ii. **Competitive advantage** - A customer-oriented approach can help you stand out in a crowded market, giving you a competitive advantage over other businesses.

iii. **Better brand reputation** - When customers have positive experiences with your brand, they are more likely to recommend your products or services to others, leading to a better brand reputation.

iv. **Increased revenue** - Satisfied customers are more likely to purchase additional products or services, resulting in increased revenue for the business.

v.   **Better employee morale** - A customer-oriented approach can lead to a more positive work environment, as employees feel a sense of satisfaction and purpose in delivering high-quality products or services that meet customer needs.

vi. **Career growth** - If you take care of your customer, and it benefits the organization, you can expect to be recognized for the same. For you, it could mean a sense of fulfilment and achievement. If you are able to consistently keep your customer happy, it could lead to better career growth for you.

How can you be customer-oriented?

If you imbibe and practice all aspects outlined in this book, it will help create a great customer experience for your customer and establish you as being customer oriented. Examples include:

i. Delivering top-notch quality.

ii. Delivering on time, every time.

iii. Going the extra mile when needed e.g., handling an urgent customer request by working extra hours.

iv. Acting as a technical and/or functional consultant, providing recommendations to customers.

v. Responding quickly to customer queries, on or before timelines agreed with them.

Note: Consistency is a crucial aspect of customer centricity. Providing quality service on time or responding quickly occasionally may create a short-term positive experience, but it is not enough to make a lasting impact. To create superior, meaningful, and memorable customer experiences, these traits must be consistently exhibited over time. That leads to deeper engagement and a customer relationship that moves beyond a mere transactional one to a more consultative and trusted partnership.

It is also worth noting that building customer trust takes time, but it can be lost quickly. Therefore, it is essential to take all necessary measures to maintain customer trust and prevent any erosion of that trust.

SUMMARY

Elevating customer experiences is not just about meeting expectations; it is about surpassing them at every opportunity. By understanding that the customer is at the heart of your business, you unlock a myriad of benefits, from increased satisfaction and loyalty to competitive advantage and revenue growth.

But being customer-oriented is not a one-time effort; it is a continuous journey of improvement and adaptation. It requires a commitment to delivering top-notch quality, consistently meeting deadlines, and going above and beyond when necessary. It means being a trusted advisor to the customer, responding promptly to inquiries, and always striving for excellence.

Remember, building customer trust takes time, but it can be destroyed in an instant. So, stay vigilant, maintain consistency, and never lose sight of the fact that your customers are the lifeblood of your organization. By prioritizing their needs and delivering exceptional experiences, you not only ensure their satisfaction but also pave the way for your own success and growth.

Self-Reflection

i.   *In the last customer appreciation, what were the traits that the customer appreciated about me and my work?*

ii. *How do I ensure that my customer gets the best possible experience while working with me?*

11.

ART OF SWIFT RESPONSIVENESS

Let us revisit the pizza delivery scenario discussed earlier in this book. Imagine you ordered a pizza, but it is delayed, and you are trying to call the customer care number to find out why. You have called three times, but there is no response from the other side. How would you feel? Most likely, you'd feel frustrated, annoyed, and possibly even angry. The lack of response would make you perceive the company's customer service as poor and may cause you to lose trust in their ability to provide timely and satisfactory service.

Being prompt in responding to customers is similar to participating in a table tennis match. It is a dynamic game where swift reactions are crucial to returning your opponent's shots; otherwise, you risk missing the ball. While it is impractical to be constantly monitoring your inbox, it is essential to possess the self-discipline to answer your stakeholders on the same day or, at the latest, within one business day.

In the tempo of swift response, opportunities unfold, and challenges transform.

I have encountered several reasons from people justifying their inability to respond promptly to customers, some of which are listed below:

    i.   They do not have full information requested by the customer.

    ii.   They need time to consolidate the data requested by the customer.

    iii.   They were not available to respond.

    iv.   They will respond when they have completed the requested task.

    v.   They were busy with other, high priority tasks.

At times, it is completely acceptable to not possess all the information your stakeholder is seeking right away. In such instances, the crucial step is to promptly communicate this to them, preventing them from waiting for your response and speculating about the situation at your end. A sample response is provided below:

"Thanks for your email. I am working on the information you have requested. It might take a day for me to consolidate that. Please expect a response by tomorrow morning your time."

In case you are unavailable for any reason, it is important to set up an out-of-office message that includes the contact information your stakeholder can reach out to. This will ensure that your stakeholder can still get the required help, even when you are not available. A sample response below:

"Thanks for your email. I am out of office from [this date] to [this date]. Please contact [name (email address)] in my absence for any support."

Benefits of responding swiftly

i.   **Establish trust and credibility -** Providing swift responses to requests is a crucial method of establishing trust and credibility with your stakeholders.

ii. **Better engagement** - It improves their perception of the quality of service you provide, leading to stronger engagement.

iii. **Helps maintain relationships** - It demonstrates that you are always available to assist them. This can work wonders in creating and maintaining strong relationships.

iv. **Better customer experience** - Lesser waiting time for a customer to get a response to their query or issue resolution enhances their experience of working with you.

What are the ways you can respond swiftly?

i. **Understand expectations** - Responding swiftly is subjective and open to interpretation. Try understanding from your stakeholders how long they are willing to wait for you to respond to them. Typically, 1 business day would be acceptable to most people as a turnaround time to respond to non-critical queries.

ii. **Set expectations** - If the expectations are too high, for example, if the customer wants you to respond to their queries on the same day, set reasonable expectations with them (unless responding on the same day is part of the agreement/contract), explaining why you will not be able to adhere to their expectations and why what you are proposing is more sustainable. Do cater to urgent requests though, on a need basis.

iii. **Adhere to those expectations** - Once you have agreed on a timeline by when you will respond, adhere to those timelines to build, and maintain trust with customers.

iv. **Send acknowledgements** - Even if you do not have an answer or solution to a customer query or problem, do acknowledge their email within the agreed timelines. Share an expected time by when you can get back with a response to their query or resolve their issue. Keeping the customer in dark without any timelines can make them anxious and dent their experience of working with you.

Below are a few scenarios comparing a slow approach to respond vs. prompt responsiveness for your customers:

Sub-Optimal Responsiveness	Prompt Responsiveness
Customer shares the data with you, and you start working on it.	Customer sends the data, and you thank and acknowledge them for sending the data. You also let them know that you will get back with any questions or clarifications the next day.
Customer asks a question which requires some analysis. You are busy with another urgent deliverable for the same client and cannot take it up for the next 2 days.	You acknowledge the customer email and update them that the request will take time as you are caught up in another urgent task for them. Ask them if you need to reprioritize activities to deliver this request before others.
Customer highlights issue in a deliverable and you start looking into it.	You respond to the customer saying that you are looking into the issue and will get back as soon as possible, and *then* start looking into it. Also provide a turnaround time, if possible, for getting back, and proactively keep them updated in case there is any change to the timelines.

Customer appreciates you in the call or email and you are unsure of how to respond.	You acknowledge and thank the customer for the appreciation. You can indicate that it made your day or that it means a lot to you.

SUMMARY

Mastering the art of swift responsiveness is paramount in a fast-paced business environment. Prompt responses to customers build trust, credibility, and satisfaction. Setting clear expectations, adhering to agreed timelines, and providing acknowledgments even when you are unable to immediately address an issue are essential strategies. By embracing swift responsiveness, you not only enhance customer experience but also nurture strong and enduring relationships that are fundamental to **your career** success.

Self-Reflection

i.   *How long do I generally take to respond to a customer's or colleague's emails?*

ii. *Do they have to follow-up to elicit a response from me?*

12.

THINKING BEYOND THE SELF

If you look at various levels in an organization, you will typically find the following structure:

Organization > Division > Function > Team > Self

To contribute beyond oneself means making a difference at levels other than self, such as team, function, division, or organization. By contributing at various levels in your organization, you will have the opportunity to collaborate with individuals outside your team. This experience will expose you to diverse personalities and situations, and add to your knowledge and experience, often without you even realizing it.

When you are working on initiatives outside your team, it is important to keep your manager informed of your contributions and get feedback from the lead you are working with on the initiative. Share the feedback with your manager for their information.

True fulfilment lies not just in personal success, but in the echoes of our contributions resonating beyond ourselves.

Example

One of my team members wanted to contribute beyond his role. He was a sociable person and enjoyed engaging with others. He eagerly offered to join the new employee onboarding team and made significant contributions by attending meetings, actively participating, and sharing his insights. His involvement had a noticeable positive impact on the team, resulting in outstanding feedback for him, which was considered during his year-end performance evaluation.

What are the advantages of contributing beyond self?

i. **Better team bonding and network** - If you are supporting other team members with their projects, it will lead to a better team camaraderie. When you work with people outside your team, you build new connections that you can leverage later in your career.

ii. **Enhances learning** - Different people have distinctive styles of working. You will learn new ways of working when collaborating with different people and navigating through various situations. You will also get a good view of a variety of projects outside your team.

iii. **Builds more advocates** - By demonstrating strong work ethics and superior work quality, you can build more advocates for yourself in the workplace.

iv. **Opens career opportunities** - The project that you are taking up outside your team might become your next project, and that team might be your new team. In case you are looking for role change, such projects are an opportunity for your prospective manager to see the value you bring to the table, and for you to get a view of the environment in your prospective team.

How can you contribute beyond your own work?

i. **Let your manager know** - Inform your manager about your willingness to make contributions that extend beyond your individual projects. Your manager should be able to recognize potential opportunities for you within the team. Additionally, they can inform you about any opportunities they are aware of at the functional, divisional, or organizational level.

ii. **Watch out for internal function or company emails/ newsletters** – Emails and newsletters typically contain extensive information about the organization's ongoing or upcoming activities. This will provide insights into initiatives that excite you and that you would like to engage in and support. Occasionally, these communications may also include contact details for project leads or initiative organizers, allowing you to reach out and express your interest in contributing to those initiatives.

iii. **Raise your hand** - If another team seeks assistance and you are interested in contributing, volunteer yourself by expressing your willingness.

Note: Based on my experience, there are numerous opportunities available for demonstrating contribution beyond self, ranging from minor responsibilities like being a mentor to a new joiner or scheduling team meetings to more significant tasks such as conducting training sessions for a department or overseeing company-wide events like community service or sports events. As mostly these activities will be additional to your regular project work, I recommend that you pursue these opportunities aligned with your interest and passion. That way, there will be a high chance of you participating wholeheartedly and doing justice to your nomination for the initiative.

When passion meets profession, work becomes a joyful journey.

Also, always be aligned with your manager before committing yourself to other assignments. This will avoid any conflicting assignments in case your manager has already planned something else for you.

SUMMARY

The journey of contributing beyond oneself is a fundamental aspect of career growth and personal fulfilment. By embracing opportunities to make a difference at various levels within the organization, you can enrich your professional journey as well as your workplace environment. Strengthening networks, cultivating advocates, and gaining diverse experiences are just some of the benefits that await you if you extend your reach beyond immediate responsibilities.

However, this journey requires thoughtful navigation and alignment with organizational objectives. Open communication with your manager ensures that your contributions resonate with the overarching goals of your organization while minimizing the risk of conflicting assignments. As you embark on this path, you will not only elevate your own career but also contribute to a culture of collaboration, innovation, and collective success within the organization.

Self-Reflection

i.   *When was the last time I contributed to something beyond my project? What did I learn?*

ii. *How do I feel about contributing and supporting others in their projects?*

13.

CURIOSITY UNLEASHED

Being curious in the workplace means having a strong desire to learn, explore and understand new things. It involves asking questions, seeking out new information, and being open to new ideas and perspectives. The ability to ask questions and seek knowledge can help you significantly in your professional life. When you are curious, you have a desire to learn and understand better. Good managers expect their employees to be curious and have a desire to learn.

Curiosity is the spark that fuels your journey from what you know to what you could become.

Example

One of my team members was tasked with developing a new tool for the team's onboarding process. As he began researching different approaches, he stumbled upon a new technology that he had not worked with before. Intrigued, he dug deeper and found that this technology had the potential to not only solve the problem at hand but also improve other processes.

Instead of simply implementing the feature as assigned, he took the initiative to explore this new technology further. He reached out to colleagues who had experience with it and built expertise on this technology. His curiosity led him to discover an innovative solution that ended up significantly improving the process and even earning recognition from the function head.

In this example, the team member's curiosity motivated him to go beyond the original task and explore new possibilities. This ultimately led to a successful outcome that benefited the function as well as him.

How can being curious at the workplace help?

i. **Increases learning and effectiveness** - Curiosity helps new joiners to seek out new knowledge and understanding, which can aid in their learning process and help them to become more knowledgeable about their work and the company. By being curious, you can also gain a deeper understanding of the work you do. You can learn about the industry, the competition, and the latest trends. This knowledge can help you make informed decisions and be more effective in your role.

ii. **Value addition** - Better knowledge and improved effectiveness will help you add value to your clients and colleagues.

iii. **Builds relationships** - By showing a genuine interest in your colleagues and the company, and being able to add value to them, you can build strong relationships with your peers and superiors, which can help you navigate the workplace more effectively.

iv. **Fosters personal growth** - Being curious allows you to challenge yourself and develop new skills, which can lead to personal and professional growth and advancement.

v. **Improves problem-solving** - Curious individuals tend to be better problem-solvers, as they are constantly seeking out new information and perspectives that can help them approach challenges in a more effective way.

How can you demonstrate curiosity?

i. **Ask questions** - When you are starting a new job or role, take advantage of the opportunity to ask lots of questions during onboarding and training. This is a time when it is completely normal to seek clarification and gain a deeper understanding of the topics covered. Do not be afraid to ask as many questions as you need to feel confident in your work.

ii. **Understand the 'why'** - In the workplace, the emphasis is usually on the "what" and "how" of doing things, but it is equally important to understand the "why" behind them. From my experience, I have noticed that many employees overlook this aspect. Hence, when you are given a project, take the initiative to ask for the business context behind it. For example, why is the client making changes in the business rules every quarter in your project? Or why is there a restructuring at the client's end? Understanding the 'why' project will enable you to deliver your best and accomplish the project objectives effectively.

iii. **Clarify abbreviations** - At the workplace, colleagues may use abbreviations when discussing topics with you, assuming you are familiar with them. However, it is okay to ask them to explain the meaning of an abbreviation you do not understand.

iv. **Read widely** - Expanding your reading across diverse subjects is instrumental in enhancing your knowledge and global awareness. It introduces you to fresh concepts and viewpoints that might remain undiscovered otherwise. Cultivate a strong reading routine early in your career, emphasizing learning and understanding over the quantity of reading. Concentrate on extracting meaningful insights from each book or article and consider how you can apply them in both your personal and professional spheres. If you are able to discover even one or two takeaways that will stay with you for your lifetime, it was a worthy read.

v. **Challenge assumptions** - Questioning assumptions with a positive purpose is a key aspect of curiosity. Instead of accepting things at face value, inquire about the reasons behind them and explore potential alternatives. Pay attention to the manner in which you pose questions or challenge others to avoid coming across as impolite or offensive.

vi. **Clarify industry jargon** - Depending on the business and industry, there might be specific terms or jargon that is commonly used, which may be unfamiliar to you. It is important not to hesitate in asking questions to gain a better understanding of these terms. This will help expand your knowledge base, enable you to handle queries effectively and empower you to assist others in understanding these terms better.

vii. **Connect with others** - Curiosity is often sparked by conversations with others. Connect with people from different backgrounds and perspectives to learn new things and expand your knowledge.

Note: While being curious is a good trait, do not overdo it to make it your weakness. Sometimes new, or even existing employees will ask so many questions that it looks weird. They would ask questions after every statement from the presenter/trainer to the extent that it becomes an interruption in the flow of the session. Be mindful: ask questions in moderation. Excess of anything is harmful. If you genuinely have too many questions, you can make a note and clarify at a later point in time, separately, with the concerned person.

SUMMARY

Embracing curiosity in the workplace is not just about seeking answers; it is about embarking on a journey of self-discovery and growth. By nurturing curiosity, you pave the way for continual learning, enhanced problem-solving abilities, and enriched relationships with peers and superiors. The practical steps outlined - from asking questions and understanding the 'why' behind tasks to reading widely and challenging assumptions - serve as a roadmap for cultivating curiosity effectively. It is the curious minds that propel innovation and drive progress in the ever-evolving landscape of the professional world.

Self-Reflection

i. *How often do I actively seek out new knowledge and understanding in my professional environment?*

ii. *Am I consistently curious about improving my skills and learning about industry trends?*

iii. *How would I approach if my manager assigns me a task to be completed that I do not clearly understand?*

14.

POWER OF BEING INSPIRED AT WORK

Being inspired at the workplace is about feeling a sense of passion and purpose towards one's work. It is the feeling of being motivated, energized, and enthusiastic about the job, and having a strong desire to achieve one's goals. It is about finding meaning in the work that is being done and feeling a sense of fulfilment and accomplishment.

Example

I have observed individuals who exhibit a strong passion for their work taking complete ownership and responsibility for their assigned tasks. They are highly collaborative and always ready to assist others. They prioritize maintaining a high standard of quality in their work and feel a sense of responsibility if any mistakes occur, striving to prevent them from recurring. They consistently endeavour to ensure excellent customer experiences and are willing to go above and beyond to achieve customer satisfaction. They take the initiative to improve their team or function, connecting with the organization's vision and mission, and seeking to contribute towards achieving them. They act as role models for other team members, serving as an inspiration for others.

How does it help to be inspired at workplace?

i. **Creates positive impact** - When you are truly inspired, it is easy for others to recognize that. You gradually become role model for others, positively impacting them not just at work, but personally as well.

ii. **Increases motivation** - When you are inspired, you are more motivated to work hard and achieve your goals. This can lead to better job performance and career success.

iii. **Greater job satisfaction** - Feeling inspired can make your work feel more meaningful and fulfilling. This can lead to greater job satisfaction and a more positive attitude towards work.

iv. **Enhances collaboration** - When you are inspired, you are more likely to collaborate with others and share your ideas. This can lead to better teamwork and more successful projects.

v. **Increases resilience** - Feeling inspired can help you overcome challenges and setbacks at work. It can give you the energy and determination to keep pushing forward and find new solutions.

How can you be inspired at workplace?

i. **Surround yourself with positive people and experiences** - Seek out opportunities to learn and grow and collaborate with colleagues who share your passion and enthusiasm. When you work in an environment that supports and encourages you, it can be easier to stay inspired and motivated. Be mindful of people who keep cribbing all the time.

ii. **Set goals** - Having clear and specific goals can help you stay on track to achieve them. Make sure your goals are challenging but attainable.

iii. **Seek out challenges** - Take on new challenges and projects that push you out of your comfort zone. This can help you develop new skills and stay motivated.

iv. **See the bigger picture** - Seeing the bigger picture can serve as a powerful source of inspiration in the workplace by providing you with a sense of purpose, clarity, and motivation.

v. **Seek inspiration from role models** - Identify individuals within or outside your organization who inspire you. Learn from their experiences, achievements, and leadership styles. Their success stories can serve as a strong source of inspiration.

vi. **Take breaks** - Sometimes taking a break from your work can help you feel refreshed and re-energized. Take a short walk or engage in a relaxing activity to clear your mind.

Being inspired can create a virtuous cycle of inspiration where individuals are motivated to achieve greater levels of success and fulfilment. When individuals feel inspired, they are more likely to engage in behaviors that help them achieve their goals and push past their limits. This, in turn, can create a sense of accomplishment and confidence, leading to even more inspiration and motivation to achieve greater things.

Inspiration can come from many sources, including leaders, co-workers, and even the work itself. When individuals are inspired by their work, they are more likely to approach it with enthusiasm and a sense of purpose. They may be more creative and innovative in their problem-solving, and they may be more willing to take risks to try new approaches.

Leaders can play an important role in inspiring their team members. When leaders communicate a clear vision and purpose of the work that their team is doing, they can help team members see the impact of their work and feel a sense of pride in their contributions. Leaders who are themselves inspired by the work can also create a contagious enthusiasm that can inspire others to reach for greater heights.

To create a culture of inspiration in the workplace, it's important for leaders to encourage and recognize inspiration in their team members. This can include acknowledging accomplishments, providing opportunities for growth and development, and creating a supportive and positive work environment. It is also important for individuals to seek out sources of inspiration and actively cultivate their own sense of motivation and enthusiasm.

Remember, that leadership is not about designation. You can be a leader too for someone in your organization. So be inspired and inspire others.

SUMMARY

The power of being inspired at work cannot be overstated. When you are inspired, you become a beacon of positivity, influencing not only your own performance but also uplifting those around you.

Inspiration breeds success, and as a leader - whether by title or influence - you have the power to inspire those around you. By nurturing a culture of inspiration and recognizing its importance, both individuals and organizations can achieve greater heights of success and fulfilment.

i. *How can I find and maintain a sense of inspiration in my daily work, and what specific steps can I take to foster this feeling consistently?*

ii. *In what ways can I influence and inspire my colleagues and team members through my actions and attitude at work?*

15.

EMBRACING FEEDBACK

Embracing feedback means being open and receptive to feedback from others. It involves absorbing feedback without getting defensive or making excuses and using it to improve oneself and one's work. Being receptive to feedback requires being willing to acknowledge one's strengths, weaknesses, and areas for improvement, and being open to learning from others.

I would rate openness or receptivity to feedback as one of the critical ways to learn, grow and be a better person and professional. When we talk about feedback, it encompasses both positive feedback, which is more about what you are doing well, but also the constructive feedback which will highlight areas for improvement and development, leading to your growth. Everyone will react to positive and developmental feedback in different ways.

Embracing feedback is not just a willingness to listen; it is a commitment to personal and professional evolution.

What are the different typical reactions to feedback?

Based on my experience, I have observed that people react to feedback in many ways. They could:

i.   Be open to positive feedback but unwilling to accept feedback on areas of improvement due to a lack of self-awareness.

ii. Be open to positive feedback, and aware of areas of improvement, but often cite external factors beyond their control for why they are not good at something.

iii. Be open to both positive feedback and areas of improvement, indicating a willingness to improve.

iv. Attribute success and positive feedback to external factors (being humble), and also open to feedback on areas for improvement.

v. Accept positive feedback and *actively seek* to understand their areas of improvement.

Broadly speaking, the first two responses come from individuals who shy away from constructive feedback. They will be in a denial mode for their development areas and delude themselves into being 'perfect' or finding reasons to justify their areas of development, hindering their growth. Either of the last three responses will come from individuals who are receptive to developmental feedback, are willing to work on it and improve and evolve as better professionals.

Managers of individuals who resist constructive feedback might limit their feedback to what is strictly necessary for their job performance, showing less investment in the individual's growth. Conversely, for employees who are receptive to constructive feedback, managers are more likely to provide ongoing feedback and be dedicated to supporting their professional growth and development.

Who can give you feedback?

Although the common response may be "a manager," feedback can come from anyone depending on how receptive you are to it. Feedback can be requested from managers, colleagues, seniors, and even subordinates and customers. Obtaining feedback from a variety of individuals can provide insight into how different people perceive you. For instance, while seniors may provide positive feedback based on your work, juniors might suggest that you come across as harsh and unfriendly. It is up to you to reflect on whether or not you want to be perceived that way by your juniors and what steps you can take to improve yourself.

How can you ask for feedback?

A simple way of asking feedback is:

- *What do I do well and can continue to do?*

- *What can I start doing?*

- *What can I stop doing?*

- *What can I do differently?*

You can ask these questions to anyone you want to get feedback from. You can also ask for feedback on specific areas. For example:

- *What are your thoughts on my communication?*

- *How is the quality of my work?*

- *How can I better manage my time and prioritize tasks?*

- *What do you think about my ability to work collaboratively with others?*

Or you can ask for general feedback like:

- *Am I able to meet your expectations?*

- *What areas you would like me to focus on in the future?*

- *What suggestions do you have for me to enhance my professional development?*

- *What can I do to better support the team or organization?*

What are the advantages of being open to feedback?

i.   **Improved performance** - Feedback helps individuals understand the expectations of their supervisors or colleagues, leading to better alignment of goals and objectives. Receiving feedback can help individuals identify and correct their mistakes, which can improve their performance and productivity.

ii. **Personal and professional growth** - Feedback allows individuals to identify areas of improvement and work towards personal and professional growth. By actively seeking feedback and accepting it positively, individuals can learn new skills and develop their strengths, which can lead to career advancement.

iii. **Strengthened relationships** - When individuals are open to feedback, it shows their willingness to listen and learn from others. This can strengthen relationships with colleagues, supervisors, and customers, leading to better collaboration and teamwork.

iv. **Increased job satisfaction** - Feedback can help individuals feel valued, cared for, and appreciated, leading to increased job satisfaction. It also provides a sense of direction and purpose, which can boost motivation and engagement.

v.   **Better decision-making** - Feedback can provide individuals with different perspectives and insights, helping them make better decisions. This can lead to better outcomes for the individual, team, and organization as a whole.

What should you consider while receiving feedback?

i.   **Listen actively** - When someone shares feedback with you, listen attentively without interrupting. Show that you are interested in their perspective by maintaining eye contact and nodding.

ii. **Avoid being defensive** - Avoid becoming defensive when receiving feedback, even if you do not agree with it. Instead, ask questions to clarify and understand their perspective.

iii. **Express appreciation** - Thank the person for their feedback, even if it is negative. Acknowledge that it takes courage to provide feedback and express gratitude for their honesty.

iv. **Keep an open mind** - Be open to different opinions and perspectives. Avoid judging or dismissing feedback without consideration.

v. **Follow-up** - After receiving feedback, follow up with the person to let them know how you plan to address their concerns or use their feedback to improve.

vi. **Be proactive** - Instead of waiting for feedback, proactively ask for it. Create a culture where feedback is encouraged and valued, and actively seek out opportunities for improvement.

Note: While your manager and superiors will be more open in giving you feedback - both positive and developmental, your peers and subordinates may not be comfortable in sharing constructive feedback with you. And not all organizations may have a formal mechanism of seeking feedback from peers and subordinates. Therefore, you can look for creative ways to actively seek feedback when formal mechanisms of obtaining feedback are unavailable. For example, you can ask one of your mature team members to consolidate feedback from everyone in your team on what you can start doing, stop doing and continue to do. They can share the feedback anonymously with you. You will need to assure your team members of the anonymity so that they can share their feedback openly, which is also dependent on the trust and relationship you have with them.

Feedback should be valued and appreciated like a gift, even if it is not always easy to accept. It can help you improve and grow, and it shows that the giver cares about your development and success. Therefore, it is important to receive feedback graciously and with an open mind, and to use it to make positive changes in your behavior or work.

Another aspect to be noted is that many of us are not trained to respond to positive feedback. I have seen people simply continuing with the discussion without acknowledging or responding to positive feedback. Below are a few ways to respond to positive feedback from customers or colleagues:

"I genuinely appreciate your positive feedback. Thank you for taking the time to share your thoughts."

"I'm glad to hear that you found my work on [specific project/task] valuable. It means a lot to know that my efforts are recognized."

"Thank you for your kind words. I could not have achieved [specific accomplishment] without the support of my team. Their collaboration was instrumental in our success."

"Thank you for your kind words. Your feedback will motivate me to continue to give the best in my work."

SUMMARY

Embracing feedback is akin to embracing the roadmap to improvement. It is not just about being receptive to what others have to say, but rather a commitment to continuous improvement. Feedback comes in various forms, from the praise of strengths to the constructive critique of weaknesses, and how we react to it shapes our development trajectory. While some may shy away from acknowledging areas for improvement, others seize every opportunity to learn and grow. This chapter underscored the significance of being open to feedback, not only from managers but from peers, subordinates, and even clients, recognizing that each perspective offers valuable insights into our professional personas. By actively seeking feedback, graciously receiving it, and using it to drive positive change, we pave the way for enhanced performance, strengthened relationships, and ultimately, a fulfilling career journey.

Self-Reflection

i. *How did I react the last time I was given a positive or constructive feedback by my customer or supervisor?*

ii. *What is my approach to getting feedback from people I work with on a day-to-day basis apart from my manager?*

16.

UNLEASHING CREATIVITY AND INNOVATION

Creativity and innovation are related concepts but have different meanings. Creativity refers to the ability to generate new and original ideas or concepts, and to use imagination to come up with solutions to problems. Creativity involves thinking outside the box and exploring different perspectives and possibilities. Innovation, on the other hand, is the process of taking a creative idea and turning it into a practical and valuable solution. It involves transforming ideas into something that is useful and valuable to others. Innovation involves implementing new and improved processes, products, or services, and can result in a positive change or improvement in an organization or society.

In the realm of innovation, creativity is your passport. Dare to think differently and watch your career soar.

Based on my experience, I have observed that in order to be creative and innovative, two things are required: first, having a creative mindset and second, being inspired to implement creative ideas for the betterment of self, team, function, or organization. As a new joiner, you may have an advantage that you will not be influenced by the biases or preconceptions that already exist within the organization. Therefore, you can introduce novel ideas and perspectives on how tasks can be accomplished differently.

Companies are increasingly seeking creativity and innovation in a world which is changing at a pace never seen before. Therefore, it is essential for you to think beyond the conventional and be willing to share your ideas. Even small ideas can have a significant impact on the organization. If you work in the technology industry, you can as well leverage technology to explore new possibilities and drive innovation.

Examples

A few stories where I have seen employees share new ideas include:

i. **Team meeting leader** - An example of how we made changes in our team meetings is as follows: previously, the team leader would lead the meetings and do most of the talking. However, one team member suggested that team members should take turns to lead meetings and develop their leadership skills. This suggestion was implemented, and it led to more engaged team meetings.

ii. **Personalized emails** - Generally, the email from leadership with functional/ organizational updates used to be a mass email, and many associates would ignore it. One idea from an associate was to personalize emails by addressing the recipients in the salutation. This made the email more engaging for employees.

iii. **Automation** – Using new technologies, many manual processes like consolidation of ideas, reward nominations, automated reminders to get something done by the team etc. were streamlined leading to saving of manual effort.

iv. **Business ideas** - There are many other ideas on how businesses can evolve with changing technological landscape. Like a new way of marketing (digital) or a new approach to selling (personalized) or new KPIs to measure the changing business dynamics (digital adoption). While these will be domain specific, a lot of creativity and innovation is observed in emerging areas.

    v. **Generative AI use-cases –** This is the most talked about of all the technology innovations. Businesses across industries are trying to identify use-cases to leverage this technology to enhance and accelerate processes, realize significant productivity gains, or create better customer experiences.

How can you be more creative and innovative at workplace?

i. **Speak-up** - Many times, good ideas originate in our minds but that's where they remain. Have the courage to share your thoughts and ideas. Don't be afraid of the fear of judgement or rejection.

ii. **Do not assume** - If you are new in an organization, do not be under the impression that people already working with the organization would have thought about an idea or that you may be too new to talk about new ideas. Shed those inhibitions and share your ideas. Depending on the receptivity of your ideas by the new organization, you can decide how you want to approach this in the future. For example, if you see that your ideas are falling on deaf ears, you will naturally stop sharing your ideas but if your ideas are appreciated and implemented, then you can continue to share those in the future.

iii. **Brainstorm** - Collaborate with colleagues to brainstorm ideas and find new solutions to problems. Encourage everyone to contribute their ideas and build upon each other's thoughts.

iv. **Be inclusive** – If you see that someone is not participating in a brainstorming session or meeting, ask them explicitly to share their thoughts. More often than not, such people will bring a unique or different perspective to the discussion.

v. **Experiment** - Experiment with different methods and techniques to find what works best for you and your team. This can help you discover new and innovative ways of doing things. Don't be afraid to take risks, especially in early part of your career.

vi. **Embrace failure** - Do not be discouraged by failure. Embrace it as a learning opportunity and use it to improve and refine your ideas, or how you articulate and present them.

vii. **Be open-minded** - Be open to new ideas and perspectives, even if they challenge your own beliefs or assumptions. This can help you develop a more creative and innovative mindset.

Organizations nurture creativity and innovation in the workplace by cultivating an environment that values inventive thinking. One method employed to achieve this is through the establishment of a culture supportive of innovation. This can be observed through initiatives such as annual innovation festivals and periodic hackathons, which serve as platforms for soliciting and harnessing novel ideas from employees. Notably, standout concepts are acknowledged and advanced to drive change within the organization. As an employee, active participation in these events is encouraged to showcase your unique ideas and proposals to the wider organization. If there are no organization level initiatives centered around innovation, you can organize such innovation fests within your team. For example, we conducted an event within our group where we asked team members to present their ideas to a panel of leaders, and these leaders would 'fund' and 'invest' in shortlisted ideas, similar to a popular entrepreneurial show. This was quite an engaging and successful event with some groundbreaking ideas.

Remember, no idea should be discounted as insignificant. Should uncertainty arise regarding the viability of your idea, seeking input from your manager can provide valuable insight.

Note: When offering your ideas, it is important to recognize that not all of them may be viable given the project, team, or organizational constraints. Do not be discouraged if your ideas are not embraced or put into action. Continue sharing ideas that you think will be valuable for your team or organization. If you notice a pattern of your ideas not being implemented, discuss with your manager to gain insights into reasons behind it.

SUMMARY

The journey towards unlocking creativity and fostering innovation is both an individual and organizational endeavor of paramount importance. From the inception of novel ideas to their transformation into tangible solutions, the synergy between creativity and innovation propels personal and organizational growth. By embracing a culture that values inventive thinking and proactive engagement, you can contribute to a dynamic landscape where experimentation is celebrated, failures are embraced as opportunities for learning, and diverse perspectives converge to shape transformative initiatives. As you embark on this journey, remain steadfast in your commitment to pushing the boundaries of possibility, for it will be your efforts that will continue to drive positive change and shape your and your organization's future.

Self-Reflection

i.   *When was I appreciated for suggesting a creative solution?*

ii. *Which famous personality do I consider to be creative and innovative. What traits in them inspire me?*

17.

NAVIGATING THE COMMUNICATION LANDSCAPE

Communication at the workplace refers to the exchange of information, ideas, opinions, and feedback between individuals or groups within an organization. It involves both verbal and non-verbal methods of communication, including face-to-face conversations, emails, phone calls, instant messaging, presentations, and written reports.

Communication is critical for any employee, especially for a new employee who is just starting their career. Effective communication is necessary for you to understand others, as well as to make yourself understood. This helps in establishing strong relationships with colleagues and superiors, building trust and credibility, and fostering a positive work environment. Clear and concise communication ensures that everyone is on the same page and has a common understanding of expectations and goals.

There are different types of communication at workplace:

i. **Written communication** - This is where one has to write in order to communicate and can happen via emails or instant official chat messaging. Sometimes, it could spill over to SMS and personal instant messaging apps depending on company culture and urgency to communicate. Reports and presentations are also part of written communication. Written communication is important as it helps document the discussion and avoids any misunderstandings. For example, sending minutes of meetings for discussions on project scope and timelines. It is also helpful when people are working across different time zones and are unable to spontaneously interact verbally.

ii. **Verbal communication** - In a literal sense, verbal communication refers to oral communication with words that people speak. Some examples include one-on-one communication, meetings, town halls, etc.

iii. **Non-Verbal communication** - This can happen in written as well as verbal communication. Communication is not just about *what* to say, but also about *how* to say it. In written communication, the tone of an email, or sentence structure or choice of words are non-verbal communication. In oral communication, the tone, pitch, loudness, hand gestures, posture, eye movements and use of pauses are some examples of non-verbal communication. Non-verbal communication is as important as, and sometimes even more important than written and verbal communication, especially when it is about having a crucial conversation.

iv. **Listening** - Listening is an extremely important aspect of communication, more so in a world where there are more people to speak and share, than to halt and hear. Active listening includes being fully present in conversation, giving signals to the speaker like nodding of head, clarifying what is being said, and withholding judgement and advice. Reflect on your *'share of voice'* during or after a discussion or a meeting. Out of a thirty-minute meeting, if you ended up speaking for twenty-five minutes, you were definitely not being a great listener, unless the meeting was supposed to be that way.

Below are a few examples on how we use different aspects of communication at workplace:

i. You attend a meeting to understand project requirements from the customer - *Verbal, Listening*

ii. You document the requirements and send an email to the customer to confirm if you have captured them accurately - *Written*

iii. In a face-to-face one-on-one meeting, you ask questions to your manager to clarify doubts on a task - *Verbal*

iv. You send an email to your colleague sharing first version of the report for them to perform quality check - *Written*

v. You make an eye-contact with your manager during a conversation and nod your head acknowledging what they said - *Verbal, Listening, Non-verbal*

No one is perfect in communication, and everyone can get better at it. While communication is a vast topic, here are a few tips to strengthen your communication skills and be more effective:

i. **Reflect before expressing** - Avoid rushing to speak; take the time to organize your thoughts before articulating them. Occasionally, it can be beneficial to manage and understand your emotions before writing or speaking.

ii. **Articulate with clarity -** Pay attention to the clarity of your voice during communication. Is it distinct or coarse? Some individuals habitually clear their throats while speaking, which is generally not advisable unless there's an actual throat issue. Ensure your throat is clear before entering a meeting or conversation.

iii. **Be concise -** In a world filled with distractions, opt for brevity in your speech. Refrain from narrating lengthy stories to your audience unless it serves a specific purpose. Keep your message concise and straightforward, encouraging engagement through questions.

iv. **Confirm your audience's understanding -** After providing information or addressing inquiries from your audience, seek confirmation that your message has been effectively conveyed. Pose questions such as *"Did I clarify that for you?"* or *"Does my response address your question?"* to ensure understanding and open the door for further clarification if needed.

v. **Refrain from interruptions -** Allow others to express themselves without interruption. Make them feel heard. In the rare instance that you must interrupt, acknowledge that you are interrupting and present your point. Be careful not to interrupt repeatedly.

vi. **Non-verbal cues -** Be attentive to non-verbal communication elements, including your pace, tone, intonation (voice modulation), pauses, pitch, body language, and eye contact.

vii. **Listen actively -** Avoid formulating your response while the other person is still speaking. Let them complete their thoughts, then consider and share your response.

viii. **Clarity in expression -** Structure your thoughts in a way that is easily understandable for others. Provide context before conveying the main message and use analogies and anecdotes if necessary and appropriate.

ix. **Seek feedback -** Solicit feedback on your communication from colleagues to continually enhance your skills in this area.

x. **Self-talk -** Improve communication by mentally framing and articulating your thoughts. Use this technique for self-review, rehearsal, better articulation, and continuous improvement.

xi. **Record your speech -** Record your speech for later analysis of your strengths and areas for improvement. Ensure not to record any confidential company information on personal devices.

xii. **Leverage technology -** Explore apps that can assist in refining your written, verbal, and non-verbal communication skills, available on various app stores.

xiii. **Training sessions -** Participate in courses and training programs on communication within your organization, covering topics like 'email etiquettes' or 'how to make impactful presentations.' Implement the acquired skills in your work.

Communication is the bridge between ideas and success. Build it strong, and your career will reach new horizons.

It is crucial to maintain seamless communication with your manager consistently. They should be kept informed about your activities and any challenges you encounter. Without sharing your concerns, you should not expect your manager to address them. If you are contemplating resigning, it is advisable to adhere to professional protocol by discussing your decision with your manager face-to-face before formalizing it via email or the company's exit portal. This ensures transparency and prevents unexpected surprises for your manager.

Notes: While communicating, it is crucial to be authentic and true to yourself. Trying to be someone you are not, can backfire. So, it is important to be genuine and communicate in your own style to avoid any negative repercussions. Also, in a remote-friendly professional world, where most of us are bogged down with emails and instant messages, over-communication is generally preferable to under-communication as it maximises chances of clarity and alignment. The key is to do it effectively. Additionally, remember that you are in a corporate environment. Therefore, be mindful of your message (what you say) and its delivery (how you say it) irrespective of who you are communicating with. Even if others are not behaving or communicating professionally, have patience and maintain your composure, as communicating in a rude or aggressive tone can land you in trouble.

SUMMARY

Effective communication is the bedrock of a successful career. It is the channel through which relationships are built, understanding is fostered, and productivity thrives. By honing skills such as clarity, conciseness, and active listening, you can navigate the complex landscape of workplace communication with confidence and proficiency.

Maintaining transparent communication with managers is vital, ensuring alignment and addressing challenges effectively. Embracing authenticity in communication fosters trust and credibility, laying the groundwork for fruitful professional relationships. Be professional in your communication despite adversities. With these principles at heart, you can unlock new career opportunities and chart a course toward continued growth and success.

Self-Reflection

i. *Have I observed a difference in my preferred communication mode/ channels vs. my recipient's?*

ii. *How do I leverage non-verbal communication to convey my message?*

18.

UNLOCKING COLLECTIVE POTENTIAL THROUGH COLLABORATION

Collaboration refers to the process of individuals or teams working together towards a common goal or objective. It involves sharing ideas, knowledge, skills, and resources to achieve a specific outcome. Collaboration can take place within a team, across different departments or functions within an organization, or even between different organizations. Effective collaboration requires effective communication, mutual trust and respect, and a willingness to work together towards a shared goal.

Collaboration is the glue that binds individual strengths into a powerhouse, making the workplace greater than the sum of its parts.

Collaboration is a crucial value that all organizations require their employees to possess. However, sometimes there are individuals who are highly skilled, but they lack the ability to work collectively. Their perspective is competitive rather than collaborative. They refrain from sharing information, knowledge, and best practices with their colleagues because they believe it would reduce their 'competitive advantage' or their peers may get ahead of them. Such behavior restricts the team's potential and hinders organizational success.

Example

Let us consider a scenario where an employee found a more effective way to perform a task by leveraging technology, resulting in reducing a 6-hour manual process to a 5-minute automated job. However, the employee might choose not to share this valuable information with fellow team members. The reluctance to do so may stem from a deliberate decision, where the employee consciously withholds the information, or it may result from a passive attitude, assuming that other team members will eventually discover this on their own. Regardless of the reason, this lack of active collaboration hampers the potential impact on both the team and the organization as a whole. It is only through *active collaboration* that individuals can openly exchange ideas and knowledge, fostering collective learning and growth for the team. It is important to recognize and reward those who offer support, assist others when needed, and share information within and beyond their teams and encourage this behavior in others. This cultivates a culture of collaboration in the organization.

How can you benefit collaborating with others?

i.   **Learning** - Collaboration allows you to learn from others who have more experience and knowledge than you. It can also help you learn from people who have a different way of working from your own. This can help you improve your skills and knowledge faster.

ii. **Networking** - It helps you build relationships with others in the organization, which can be helpful for future career growth opportunities.

iii. **Exposure** - Working with different teams and departments can give you exposure to different aspects like working with a new geography, data set or stakeholders. It can also help you understand how things are managed in other teams vis-à-vis your team and provide opportunities to share what can be done better in your team or share best practices from your team with the other team.

iv. **Innovation** - When diverse, creative ideas come together, collaboration can lead to new and innovative ideas that can benefit the organization and improve processes.

v. **Self-discovery** - By working on something new with a new set of people, you may be able to discover your learning agility. This can boost your own and your leadership's confidence in you.

Considering the above, it is important to recognize the power of active collaboration and start practicing it early on, in one's career.

How can you collaborate with others at work?

i. **Acknowledge your and others' strengths** - If you are aware of your own strengths and limitations, and strengths of others, you will be able to collaborate with the right people for the right skills. Therefore, be aware of your own and others' strengths.

ii. **Ask for help when needed** - Do not be afraid to ask questions or seek help when you need it. This shows that you value the expertise of your colleagues and are willing to work collaboratively to achieve success.

iii. **Share your ideas and expertise** - Share your knowledge and ideas with your colleagues, whether through team meetings, emails, or informal conversations. This can help you build relationships and establish yourself as a valuable contributor to the team. You may also find like-minded people to work together on a common area of interest.

iv. **Be open to feedback** - Collaboration involves give-and-take, so be open to feedback from your colleagues. Take constructive criticism as an opportunity to learn and grow and use it to improve your work.

v. **Seek out opportunities to connect with colleagues** - Attend company events, join company-sponsored groups or clubs, and participate in team-building activities. This can help you get to know your colleagues on a personal level, which can make collaboration easier.

vi. **Use collaboration tools** - Many organizations use collaboration tools such as project management software, communication platforms, and file-sharing tools. Make sure you understand how to use these tools and participate actively in their use to facilitate collaboration with your colleagues.

SUMMARY

Collaboration stands as the cornerstone of unlocking collective potential within any organization. It transcends individual capabilities, harnessing diverse strengths into a unified force. By fostering effective communication, trust, and a shared vision, collaboration transforms workplaces into dynamic hubs of innovation and growth.

However, realizing the full benefits of collaboration requires a shift in mindset and behavior. You must recognize the value of sharing knowledge, supporting one another, and actively seeking opportunities to collaborate. Through a commitment to openness, willingness to learn from others, and embracing feedback, you can tap into the myriad benefits of collaboration, from accelerated learning and career growth to fostering innovation and self-discovery.

Self-Reflection

i. *How have my collaboration efforts influenced team success in the past, and what can I learn from those experiences to enhance future collaborations?*

ii. *What specific actions can I take to improve my collaborative skills and contribute more effectively to unlocking collective potential within my team or organization?*

19.

MANAGING A PORTFOLIO OF PROJECTS

Supervising a portfolio of projects implies transitioning from overseeing a single project to being accountable for the successful delivery of multiple projects. Embarking on the journey of managing a portfolio of projects marks a significant shift in your professional trajectory. As you transition from overseeing individual projects to orchestrating a multitude of them, the dynamics evolve, and so do the challenges and opportunities.

As you grow professionally, your sphere of management and impact expands. Envision being engrossed in your own projects, responsible for quality, timeliness, and client satisfaction. Now, imagine yourself contributing to multiple projects or orchestrating projects for a team of, let us say, ten individuals. Instantly, you are entrusted with overseeing all these facets of quality, timeliness, and client satisfaction across numerous projects. The panorama broadens significantly as you transition from an individual contributor to a project manager or team leader.

In the initial phases of your career, if you were attentive, you would have noticed how your manager skilfully managed various projects and team members. By adopting similar strategies, you can enhance your effectiveness in managing a growing portfolio of work as you progress in your career.

Handling more projects is like conducting a juggling act - each project is a ball you keep in the air and avoiding dropping the ball is key.

During this phase, start also thinking about delegation. Even though we all want to make a positive impact, we sometimes get too attached to our tasks and end up doing most of them ourselves. This means that we spend much of our time on our current role and limited time working for the next. What if we could assign our current tasks to our subordinates instead? That would free up our time to take up things for the next level - supporting our manager or their manager. It will be an organic move to getting your next promotion.

Example

After working for ten years, I reduced my involvement in creating proposals directly. Instead, when a new project came up, I would involve an experienced team member in customer calls to understand their requirements together. I provided a proposal template and some past proposals to guide my team members in creating the new proposal. After they completed the proposal, I reviewed it and suggested edits as required. This approach saved me time while also providing opportunities for team members to learn how to build proposals effectively. It also helped me do away with perfection and 'my way of working.' This was not just applicable to proposals but to other activities as well like consolidating data for a data request, creating a plan for automation etc.

Below are some ways you can manage the increased scope of your responsibilities effectively:

i. **Prioritize tasks** - Make a list of tasks based on their importance and urgency and allocate time and resources accordingly.

ii. **Delegate tasks** – When you have direct reports, you can identify tasks that can be delegated to your team members and empower them to take ownership of those tasks. Devise a mechanism to get periodic updates on these tasks. For example, have a weekly meeting or a daily stand-up.

iii. **Use time management tools** - Use tools such as calendars, to-do lists, and reminders to help manage time effectively. You can use a diary and a pen or apps for this.

iv. **Manage distractions** - Limit distractions such as email, social media, and phone calls, and focus on completing tasks. This is easier said than done in the digital age. Try switching off app notifications if it helps you focus better.

v. **Take breaks** - Take regular breaks to refresh and recharge and avoid burnout. Taking a break helps not just mentally but also physically by moving around and stretching a little.

vi. **Communicate effectively** - Communicate expectations and goals clearly to team members and provide feedback and support to help them achieve success.

vii. **Continuously improve** - Continuously seek opportunities to improve processes, systems, and skills to optimize time management and achieve better results. Use technology to streamline processes.

SUMMARY

It is evident that managing a portfolio of projects is more than just a progression in title - it is a profound evolution in responsibility and strategy. From overseeing individual tasks to orchestrating a portfolio of projects, this journey demands a shift in mindset and approach. By prioritizing tasks, delegating effectively, and harnessing the power of time management tools, you can navigate the complexities of this role with finesse and efficiency.

Yet, beyond the practical strategies lies a deeper commitment to continuous improvement and effective communication. As you embark on this journey of managing a team and portfolio of projects, remember that success lies not just in the tasks accomplished, but in the growth and fulfilment experienced along the way.

Self-Reflection

i. *What is the difference between my role and my manager's role?*

ii. *How am I preparing myself to take bigger responsibilities?*

20.

THE MENTORSHIP COMPASS

A mentor is an experienced and trusted advisor who provides guidance, support, and feedback to another individual, generally termed as a 'mentee.' The mentor can be someone within the same organization or from another organization, and they may have expertise in a particular field, skillset, or experience, relevant to the mentee's career goals and aspirations.

Finding a mentor is not expected of a new employee in the organization. And no one may ask you explicitly to find a mentor. But if you want to gain from someone's journey, learnings, and experiences, it is best to find a mentor early on in your career.

A mentor is more than a guide; they are the wind beneath your wings. In their wisdom, find a lifeline to your aspirations, transforming challenges into triumphs.

When you identify someone who could potentially be your mentor, take the initiative to establish a relationship with them. This involves asking questions, seeking their guidance, and demonstrating a sincere interest in learning from them. At the same time, if you have something to share with them for their benefit, feel free to do so. It is crucial to develop a strong bond that is built on trust and mutual respect. To ensure that your mentoring relationship remains separate from your job responsibilities, I suggest finding a mentor other than your supervisor. Your manager is responsible for overseeing your performance and development, and it may be difficult to maintain a completely independent relationship with them. Furthermore, there may be instances where you need advice on how to handle a situation with your manager, making it wise to rely on someone else as your mentor.

How can I find a mentor?

Once you settle into the organization, start actively finding a mentor for yourself. Here are some tips to help you find a suitable mentor:

i. **Find someone who you admire** - Look for someone who has the qualities you admire, such as strong communication skills, leadership abilities, and industry knowledge. A good mentor should also be approachable, supportive, and willing to share their expertise and experience.

ii. **Look for someone experienced in your domain** - You can find potential mentors by looking for individuals who are experienced in your field or industry. Although it may be a bit too soon for the early stages of your career, you might consider attending industry events or joining professional groups to network and meet experienced professionals.

iii. **Use online resources** - You can look for groups or communities on social media or professional networking sites. You can also ask your current connections to help create new connections as needed.

What are the benefits of having a mentor in professional life?

i. **Career development and growth**: Your mentors can assist you with professional development, career growth, goal-setting, and overall improvement of your performance.

ii. **Sharing perspectives** - A mentor can also act as a sounding board for you, helping you navigate the complexities of the workplace and providing valuable insights and perspectives on various work-related and personal matters.

iii. **Honest feedback** – A good mentor will share honest feedback with you on your strengths as well as areas of development. You are more likely to be receptive to their feedback as it will be independent of your performance evaluation.

iv. **Nudging to get out of comfort zone** – If you have a good mentor, they will nudge you to come out of your comfort zone and do things that will really help you grow personally and professionally.

v. **Emotional support** – You are more likely to be open with your mentors if you are facing some critical situation at work. They will provide you emotional support which is essential when you are going through a rough patch in your career.

The benefits of having a mentor may not always be immediately apparent, but as you progress in your career, there will be moments when their presence and guidance will prove to be extremely valuable. Invest time in finding the right mentor for you and building and sustaining relationship with them.

Note: In modern workplaces, reverse mentoring has emerged as a transformative approach to fostering mutual learning and collaboration. Unlike traditional mentoring where senior professionals guide their junior counterparts, reverse mentoring flips the script, allowing less experienced individuals to mentor their more seasoned colleagues. This innovative concept thrives on the exchange of knowledge, particularly in areas where younger employees excel, such as technology, social media, or evolving work practices. The benefits of reverse mentoring are manifold - it enhances cross-generational understanding, promotes diversity of thought, and accelerates adaptation to contemporary trends. For those seeking to stay ahead in their careers, embracing reverse mentoring can be a strategic move, providing unique insights and fostering a culture of continuous learning, ultimately contributing to personal and professional growth.

Another point to be noted is that while mentors offer invaluable guidance and support in navigating career challenges and strategic decisions, they typically are not the appropriate resource for addressing day-to-day operational issues. Mentors primarily provide insights based on their broader experience and perspective, focusing on long-term career development rather than immediate problem-solving. For operational matters, it is more suitable to turn to supervisors, colleagues, or specific people within the organization who can provide targeted advice and solutions relevant to the current challenges you face. This distinction ensures that the mentoring relationship remains focused on strategic growth and mutual learning, preserving its effectiveness and value over time.

SUMMARY

Mentors play a crucial role in professional development. A mentor is an experienced advisor who provides guidance, support, and feedback, helping you navigate your career and achieve your goals. Building a strong, respectful relationship with a mentor can significantly enhance your professional growth and performance.

Finding a mentor involves identifying someone you admire, preferably with experience in your field, and actively seeking their guidance. Additionally, reverse mentoring, where less experienced individuals mentor their senior counterparts, can offer unique benefits by fostering mutual learning and understanding.

Embrace mentorship as a key element of your career journey, using it to gain valuable insights and support for your ongoing development.

Self-Reflection

i.   *Who amongst my seniors or leaders genuinely cares about me?*

ii. *Who can I reach out to for help with a current situation I am facing at work? Can they be my mentor?*

21.

ESSENCE OF WORKPLACE INTEGRITY

Maintaining integrity in a professional context refers to consistently upholding honesty, ethics, and moral principles in one's actions and decisions. It involves adhering to a strong moral and ethical code, being truthful and transparent, and acting in a way that is fair and just. Integrity embodies the consistent alignment of one's actions with their core values. It is the unwavering commitment to honesty, transparency, and ethical conduct, even when faced with challenges or tempting shortcuts.

Integrity is the silent architect of character, building a foundation of trust, respect, and authenticity in every choice we make.

Why is maintaining integrity important at workplace?

i. **Trust and credibility** - Integrity is fundamental to building trust among colleagues, superiors, and clients. When individuals consistently act with honesty and ethical conduct, they establish credibility, making it more likely for others to rely on their word and judgment.

ii. **Positive work culture** - Workplace integrity contributes to the creation of a positive and ethical work culture. When employees witness integrity in action, it fosters an environment of respect, cooperation, and professionalism.

iii. **Organizational reputation** - Integrity is closely tied to an organization's reputation. Companies with a strong commitment to ethical behavior and integrity are more likely to be respected by customers, partners, and the broader community. A positive reputation contributes to long-term success.

iv. **Legal and regulatory compliance** - Adhering to integrity standards ensures that individuals and organizations comply with legal and regulatory requirements. It reduces the risk of legal issues, financial penalties, and damage to the organization's standing.

How can you demonstrate integrity at workplace?

i. **Admitting mistakes** - When you make a mistake, take responsibility for it. Admitting errors and working towards solutions demonstrates accountability and integrity. It also shows that you value honesty over covering up mistakes.

ii. **Compliance with organization policies and regulations** - Adhere to company policies, industry regulations, and legal requirements. Avoid engaging in practices like bribery, which violate ethical standards or compromise the organization's integrity.

iii. **Promoting a culture of integrity** - Encourage and support a culture of integrity within your team and organization. Do not be ashamed or embarrassed of doing or supporting the right thing.

iv. **Lead by example** – Lead by example and promote ethical behavior by recognizing and rewarding employees who demonstrate integrity. This assumes even more importance when you move into a leadership role in your organization.

v. **Continuous learning** - Stay informed about ethical standards and best practices within your industry. Engage in ongoing education to enhance your understanding of ethical considerations in the workplace. Ignorance is not a valid reason for failing to uphold integrity.

Examples

I have witnessed some of my colleagues demonstrate admirable integrity within the workplace. For example, one colleague discovered an unexplained amount deposited in her bank account by the organization. Despite the modest amount, she immediately informed me, as her manager. After that, she collaborated with the human resources and finance teams to rectify the error, ensuring prompt return of the mistakenly credited amount back to the organization. Her actions underscored a remarkable commitment to integrity, as she opted to address and resolve the issue, even though she could have chosen to ignore the issue.

In a different scenario, the team identified a major quality issue by themselves approximately three months after a project had concluded. Had the team not brought it up, the customer might not even have noticed it. The discovery of this quality issue led to additional work for the team including complex situations that had to be addressed. Despite the risk of potential impact on their performance, the team prioritized integrity over personal concerns and appropriately highlighted the issue. As a manager, I expressed my appreciation for their initiative in bringing this to my attention and collaborated with the customer to address the situation in a way that was mutually acceptable. We also worked on a plan to avoid recurrence of similar issues. This serves as another outstanding example of maintaining integrity despite leading to challenging circumstances.

To sum it up, integrity is a fundamental professional attribute that positively influences both individual careers and organizational success. Beyond professional benefits, operating with integrity contributes to individual well-being, providing a sense of pride and satisfaction in one's work.

Note: Please be aware that failing to adhere to organizational integrity standards results in immediate termination of employment. Therefore, avoid any behaviors that violate company policies. I have observed employees submitting false expense claims, taking sick leave when not actually unwell, and using someone else's access card to mark their attendance despite absence from office. These actions led to immediate dismissal of those involved. Do not engage in such unethical practices under any circumstances, as no organization will tolerate such behavior.

SUMMARY

As you conclude your exploration of workplace integrity, you recognize its far-reaching impact on both your individual fulfilment and organizational excellence. It is through your collective commitment to integrity that you cultivate a culture of respect, cooperation, and professionalism. By embracing integrity as a guiding principle, you not only safeguard your reputation but also contribute to the broader culture of ethical conduct within your organization and industry.

Self-Reflection

i.   *When did I last take a stand for doing the right thing?*

ii. *Who do I consider as a role model for integrity and why?*

22.

SEIZING OPPORTUNITIES BY TAKING INITIATIVES

Taking initiatives means identifying opportunities for improvement or growth and proactively taking action to make positive changes. It implies being a self-starter to get things done, rather than someone having to ask you to do something. It involves being proactive, creative, and willing to take risks in order to achieve organizational goals.

Initiative is the spark that ignites progress. It is the force that propels us beyond the ordinary, turning ideas into action.

Example

Here is an example of an employee taking an initiative at work: As the organization was moving from growth phase to maturity phase, there was a need to bring in productivity savings. This meant that the same work had to be done by lesser resources in the future. This team member took upon him the responsibility to identify areas of productivity savings across projects in his team, ensured that clear action items were established for each of those areas, shared this with all team members, had a mechanism to monitor progress on actions, provided an update to their manager on the progress at the same time highlighting risks and challenges.

This is just one example. There could me many ideas your manager has in mind to implement in the team or function which he would have shared in forums like team meetings. You could take a lead by picking an idea that excites you, having a discussion with your manager on how you can help bring those ideas to reality, and start planning and working towards it. Not just that, you could proactively share ideas with your manager and implement them for the benefit of your team or function.

What are the advantages of taking initiatives?

i. **Increased visibility** - When you take initiatives, you get noticed by your colleagues, superiors, and even the leadership team. This increased visibility can help you stand out and pave the way for career growth opportunities.

ii. **Improved problem-solving skills** - Initiatives often involve finding solutions to problems or creating new processes. This can help you develop your problem-solving skills and think creatively.

iii. **Enhanced leadership abilities** - By taking initiatives, you learn, practice, and demonstrate leadership qualities like proactivity, self-motivation, and the ability to inspire and influence others. These qualities are highly valued in leadership positions.

iv. **Personal and professional growth** - Taking initiatives can help you step out of your comfort zone and learn new things. This can lead to personal and professional growth and help you become a well-rounded individual.

v. **Increased job satisfaction** - When you take initiatives, you have a sense of ownership and control over your work. You also have a feeling of making a meaningful contribution to your organization. This can lead to increased job satisfaction and motivation to perform well.

vi. **Creates positive impact on the organization** - Taking initiatives that result in positive changes can have a ripple effect throughout the organization. This can improve team morale, increase productivity, and ultimately benefit the organization as a whole.

How can you take initiatives?

i. **Identify inefficiencies and propose solutions** - If you notice a process that is slowing down productivity or wasting resources, you can take the initiative to propose and implement a more efficient process.

ii. **Take additional responsibilities** - If you have capacity and see an opportunity to contribute more to your team or function, you can take the initiative to volunteer for additional responsibilities or projects.

iii. **Develop new products or services** - Taking the initiative to come up with innovative ideas for new products or services can help your function stay ahead of the competition and drive growth.

iv. **Improve capabilities** - Taking the initiative to improve capabilities within the team or function (technical, functional or soft-skills), whether by organizing trainings sessions or creating communities, which can help improve the quality of deliverables and service.

v. **Mentor or coach colleagues** - Taking the initiative to mentor or coach colleagues can help improve the skills and performance of the team as a whole.

vi. **Organize activities** - This can be a great way to bring team members together and foster better communication and collaboration. Examples of team-building activities include off-site retreats, social outings, or even simple games and exercises.

Note: While taking initiatives is consistently valued, exercising caution is equally crucial to avoid taking on an excessive workload that might become overwhelming. Some individuals, in their eagerness, assume numerous responsibilities but struggle to execute any task effectively. It is imperative to engage in activities that you can manage effectively without compromising the quality of your work. If you take up too many activities but are unable to deliver anything effectively, it could adversely affect your career advancement. Thus, it is vital to concentrate not only on the quantity of activities you undertake but also on their quality, ensuring that the outcomes from these initiatives align with your manager's and the organization's expectations.

SUMMARY

Seizing opportunities by taking initiatives is not merely a career strategy but a mindset that propels both personal and organizational growth. Initiatives are the seeds of progress, sowing the path toward innovation, efficiency, and leadership. By embracing the proactive spirit of initiative, you can accelerate positive change within your teams and beyond, driving success and fulfilment in your professional journey.

The advantages of taking initiatives are manifold, ranging from increased visibility and enhanced problem-solving skills to personal and professional growth. Moreover, initiatives have a ripple effect, fostering a culture of innovation and collaboration that uplifts team morale and benefits the organization as a whole. However, it is essential to exercise caution, ensuring that initiatives undertaken align with your capacity and do not compromise the quality of work. By balancing ambition and feasibility, you can leverage initiatives as a powerful tool for career advancement and organizational excellence.

Self-Reflection

i.   *How have I contributed to my team, function, or organization beyond regular project work?*

ii.   *How did I feel about contributing to initiatives beyond my day-to-day work?*

23.

MASTERING ASSERTIVENESS

Being assertive means communicating your thoughts, feelings, and ideas in a clear and confident manner while respecting the rights and opinions of others. While no one may question you if you challenged something in the initial stages of your career, you are less likely to do so because you are new and still exploring the organization and the team environment. However, as you progress in your career, you will need to be more assertive. You should be more comfortable in challenging the status quo or sharing your thoughts openly.

It is important to note that being assertive is different from being aggressive. Understanding this difference will avoid you from landing into situations that could work against you. Being assertive involves expressing oneself in a clear, direct, and respectful manner that communicates one's needs and desires while also respecting the needs and desires of others. Assertive communication involves active listening, expressing oneself clearly and confidently, and seeking win-win solutions that benefit all parties involved.

On the other hand, being aggressive involves using a forceful, confrontational approach that seeks to dominate and coercively impose your views on others. This can involve raising one's voice, interrupting others, and using threats or insults to get one's way. While being aggressive can sometimes achieve short-term goals, it often damages relationships and can lead to long-term negative consequences.

Assertiveness is the silent power that turns intentions into impactful actions. Navigate confidently, speak with conviction, and let your assertive presence shape the path to success.

Here are some cases of how you can be assertive, without being aggressive:

i.   **Speaking up in meetings** - If you have an idea or suggestion that you think could benefit the team or project, assertively sharing it in a meeting can demonstrate your value and leadership potential.

ii. **Setting boundaries** - It is important to assertively communicate your boundaries when it comes to your workload or work hours. For example, saying no to unreasonable requests or clarifying your availability during off-hours or if you are already stretched. This will ensure you are able to do justice to what is on your plate already.

iii. **Expressing your needs** - If you need support or resources to complete a task, it is important to assertively communicate this to your manager or team members. Do not assume that asking for help will be treated as your shortcoming. If you do not ask for help, you might risk having burnout.

iv. **Giving and receiving feedback** - Providing constructive feedback to colleagues or supervisors while also being open to receiving feedback yourself can help foster a culture of growth and development.

v.   **Setting expectations** - For example, if a customer proposed a timeline which is overly aggressive and nearly infeasible, you can push the customer back giving valid reasons. Customer centricity is not about saying 'yes' to every request from them. Sometimes, you need to take a stance and be assertive and propose alternative solutions.

Example

Our team encountered challenges while assisting a customer with a project featuring quarterly deliverables. The customer consistently shared data late, leading to the team working long hours. Additionally, incomplete, or missing data during validation checks necessitated rework, impacting our efficiency.

We had already meticulously documented delays in receiving data and data quality issues. After collating three quarters' worth of data, we approached the customer positively, discussing the importance of receiving timely and complete data. The conversation, devoid of blame, resulted in a commitment from the customer to provide high-quality data on schedule. Subsequently, we observed marked improvements in data quality and timeliness, enabling the team member to better plan and manage their work.

What I want to highlight using this example is that we need not necessarily accept the status quo. If we see an opportunity for improvement, we should be assertive without seeming rude, insensitive, or aggressive.

How does it help to be assertive?

i. **Increased respect** - Being assertive can earn you the respect of your colleagues and superiors, as they see you as someone who is confident and capable.

ii. **Reduced stress** - When you are assertive, you are less likely to feel stressed or anxious about your interactions with others, as you are able to express yourself in a clear and confident manner. You may also be able to 'push-back' on unreasonable timelines and other requests.

iii. **Increased self-confidence** - When you are assertive, you are standing up for yourself and your ideas, which can boost your confidence and self-esteem.

iv. **Better decision-making** - When you are assertive, you are more likely to make decisions that are in best interests for you, your team and function, rather than simply going along with what others want.

Note: Being assertive at work requires confidence, which comes from doing a good job. If you are not performing well and delivering poor quality work, you won't have the power to be assertive. Attempting to assert yourself without meeting performance standards could verge on audacity.

Be genuine when being assertive. For example, saying 'no' to support a team member who is stretched when you actually have the capacity to support will not be appreciated. Have an objective discussion with your manager when you are not in a position to support additional requests. It is not too difficult for experienced managers to make out which team member is genuinely occupied vs. who is faking it. Actions and behavior speak a lot for an individual without they even realizing it.

SUMMARY

Being assertive is a crucial skill for navigating the complexities of the workplace with confidence and professionalism. It entails effectively communicating your thoughts, needs, and boundaries while also respecting those of others. Understanding the distinction between assertiveness and aggression is paramount, as the former fosters constructive dialogue and mutual respect, whereas the latter can lead to strained relationships and negative outcomes in the long run.

By embracing assertiveness, you can unlock numerous benefits. However, it is important to remember that genuine assertiveness stems from competence and authenticity. Strive to maintain integrity in your assertive communications, ensuring that your actions align with your capabilities and commitments. Ultimately, by mastering assertiveness, you can effectively navigate professional challenges while fostering positive relationships and achieving long-term success in your career.

Self-Reflection

i.   *How do I put forward my point of view when it is different from the other person?*

ii. *What specific steps can I take to further enhance my assertiveness skills while maintaining respectful communication with colleagues and stakeholders?*

24.

BEING ACTION ORIENTED

In a professional setting, demonstrating an action-oriented approach entails a readiness to take risks, make decisive choices, and move forward with a sense of urgency to accomplish tasks. This stands in contrast to individuals with a complacent or laid-back behavior who tend to delay tasks without justification.

Action-oriented individuals are often self-starters and can work independently with minimal supervision. They are not afraid to tackle new challenges or take on projects that are outside their comfort zone. They are also able to break down complex tasks into manageable steps and prioritize them based on their importance and urgency.

Example

One of my team members served as a notable illustration of being action oriented. Rather than waiting for task assignments, he proactively took ownership and expressed confidence in completing the task at hand. He approached work with enthusiasm, ensuring timely completion, often ahead of schedule. For longer duration projects, he maintained regular communication, updated me and relevant stakeholders on progress and potential challenges. His proactive engagement extended to reaching out to gather information and identifying key stakeholders for new business opportunities. Furthermore, he consistently contributed innovative ideas for process improvement. Having such self-driven team members who accomplish tasks with minimal guidance is a true pleasure for any manager.

What are the advantages of being action-oriented?

i. **Increases productivity** - By focusing on action and taking concrete steps towards achieving goals, you can increase your productivity and make better use of your time. This adds to the overall productivity of the organization.

ii. **Drives results** - Action-oriented individuals focus on achieving results and take steps to make things happen. This can help them achieve their goals and contribute to the success of the organization.

iii. **Enhances accountability** - When you take action, you are taking responsibility for your work and your goals. This can help you become more accountable for your actions and lead to greater success.

iv. **Builds trust and credibility** - As you consistently take action and accomplish tasks, your colleagues, managers, and customers will have a more positive experience working with you. This can result in increased opportunities and stronger relationships in the workplace. However, it is important to remain mindful that quality should never be sacrificed in the pursuit of being action oriented, as compromising on quality can ultimately be counterproductive.

How can one be action-oriented at work?

i. **Take ownership** - Take responsibility for your work. If you have to do something, do it on your own rather than someone having to remind you or following-up with you.

ii. **Be proactive** - Don't wait for others to tell you what to do; take the initiative and be proactive in seeking out opportunities to contribute and make a difference.

iii. **Follow through** - Once you have committed to a task, follow through on it and take it to completion. Uphold your commitments and do not let setbacks or obstacles deter you from achieving your goals. Highlight challenges and risks proactively, if any.

iv. **Respond quickly** - If there is a task that has a deadline, it is important to begin working on it promptly and let your stakeholders know that you have already started on it. Ensure that it is completed within the designated timeframe.

In the realm of achievement, being action-oriented is the compass that turns aspirations into reality. It's the driving force that transforms intent into impact.

Note: It is crucial not only to prioritize speed in completing tasks but also to regularly communicate their status to keep stakeholders informed of progress. Additionally, while you may initially be action-oriented upon joining an organization, it is important to avoid complacency as you acclimate to your role. As you become more acquainted with the organization, its people, and processes, there is a tendency to slip into a comfort zone, which can then lead to complacency. Stay proactive and guard against falling into these zones.

SUMMARY

In your journey of professional development, embracing an action-oriented mindset is key to unlocking success. By seizing initiative, shouldering responsibility, and actively pursuing your goals, you can bolster productivity, drive tangible results, and nurture a culture of accountability in your workplace. This approach offers numerous advantages, from fostering trust and credibility to fueling innovation. Yet, it is crucial to balance action with quality and effective communication to avoid potential pitfalls.

To cultivate an action-oriented ethos, prioritize taking ownership of tasks, seeking out opportunities, and committing to seeing them through to completion. Stay proactive, responsive to challenges, and guard against complacency by remaining vigilant. By embodying the spirit of action, you empower yourself to realize your full potential, leaving a lasting impact on your career and the organizations you serve.

Self-Reflection

i. *When did I demonstrate a sense of urgency to get something done?*

ii. *How did I feel about going through the experience of a service provider being slow in resolving my issue?*

25.

NAVIGATING WITH EMOTIONAL INTELLIGENCE

Emotional intelligence refers to the ability to understand and manage one's own emotions and to recognize and respond to the emotions of others. It involves being aware of one's own feelings and reactions, managing one's emotions in a healthy way, empathizing with others, and effectively communicating and collaborating with others. As you move to the later part of your initial career, these skills become crucial as your role will evolve from managing yourself to managing others. Even if you are an individual contributor and not directly managing others, you will be working with many more people now than before. For instance, you may be a project manager working with people who report to other managers.

In the age of artificial intelligence, one of the most important skills required when working with people is emotional intelligence. Emotional intelligence helps leaders create a positive and supportive work environment, leading to increased employee engagement, job satisfaction, and productivity.

Example

Here is an example of display of emotional intelligence: for one of the team members, one of their parents had unexpectedly passed away. This led to the team member being in a state of shock for an extended period of time, more than one would typically expect. It also impacted the team member's availability and effectiveness once they resumed work.

As a leader, it is important to understand that losing a parent is an exceedingly difficult and emotional experience. It can bring about a range of emotions such as sadness, grief, anger, confusion, and a feeling of being lost or alone. The intensity and duration of these emotions can vary depending on the individual and their relationship with their parent. It is normal to feel overwhelmed and to need time to process and come to terms with the loss of a loved one.

It may be necessary for the individual to take some time off professionally to attend to personal matters. Employers and colleagues can show empathy and support during this difficult time by offering condolences and providing necessary assistance to help the individual cope with the loss. This emotional intelligence in the manager helped to give some space and time to the associate to recover from the extreme loss.

A sub-optimal thing to do here would have been to expect the associate to take the "standard" time to recover from such a personal loss. Expecting the associate to be back to normal and work fully effectively would have been insensitive and shown lack of emotional intelligence. The associate would have been scarred by this insensitivity for his lifetime.

Unlike machines, humans possess the invaluable essence of a heart, driving emotions, empathy, and the intricate nuances of the human experience, making us inherently unique in the realm of artificial intelligence.

What are the advantages of exhibiting emotional intelligence?

i. **Effective communication** - Leaders with emotional intelligence have better communication skills, which helps them to understand the needs and concerns of their team members and respond appropriately.

ii. **Empathy and compassion** - Leaders with emotional intelligence are better able to empathize with their team members and are more compassionate and supportive. This can lead to increased job satisfaction, loyalty, and productivity.

iii. **Improved decision-making** - Emotional intelligence enables leaders to make better decisions by taking into account the emotions and feelings of their team members, as well as the broader impact of their decisions.

iv. **Better self-awareness** - Leaders with emotional intelligence have a better understanding of their own emotions and behaviors, allowing them to regulate their own emotions and respond appropriately to different situations.

If a leader lacks emotional intelligence, they may struggle to effectively manage their own emotions, as well as those of their team members. This can lead to a number of negative consequences, including:

i. **Poor communication** - A leader who lacks emotional intelligence may struggle to communicate clearly and effectively with their team members. They may not be able to understand or empathize with their team members' perspectives, which can lead to misunderstandings, miscommunications, and conflicts.

ii. **Low morale** - When a leader is unable to connect with their team members on an emotional level, it can lead to low morale and a lack of motivation among team members. This can lead to decreased productivity and poor performance.

iii. **High turnover** - Employees who feel that their emotional needs are not being met by their leader or organization may become disengaged and eventually leave the organization. This can lead to high turnover rates, which can be costly for the organization.

iv. **Difficulty managing stress** - A leader who lacks emotional intelligence may struggle to manage stress and may be prone to becoming overwhelmed or reactive in high-pressure situations. This can lead to poor decision-making and ineffective leadership.

How can one be more emotionally intelligent?

i. **Practice self-awareness** - Pay attention to your own emotions, how they impact your behavior and actions, and how others perceive you.

ii. **Respond, don't react** - Control your emotions and avoid impulsive reaction. Learn how to manage stress and remain calm in difficult situations.

iii. **Practice empathy** - Put yourself in others' shoes and try to understand their perspectives and emotions. Be respectful and considerate towards others, even if you don't agree with them.

iv. **Be an active listener** - Pay attention to what others are saying, show interest in their thoughts and opinions, and ask clarifying questions.

v. **Read literature** - There are many books and articles available on this topic. Since emotional intelligence will be a critical skill as you move ahead in your career, an early start to the concepts and conscious practice will help you in the long term.

Organizations recognize the importance of emotional intelligence and often take steps to improve employees' emotional quotient (EQ). In any organization, emotional intelligence is particularly important for leaders as they engage with multiple employees and play a critical role in inspiring and motivating them.

Note: A prevalent illustration of demonstrating emotional intelligence is when you receive an email that elicits negative emotions in you. Instead of reacting impulsively, take a moment to compose yourself. Consider whether it is prudent to respond in writing or if a conversation with the sender would be more effective in conveying your perspective and addressing any concerns about the email's content. This cautious approach is essential because written communication is permanent, necessitating careful consideration of the message conveyed.

SUMMARY

It is imperative to recognize the indispensable role emotional intelligence plays in shaping one's professional trajectory. Through an exploration of concepts such as self-awareness, empathy, and adept communication, a profound understanding of essential tools for success emerges. Equipped with the acumen of emotional intelligence, adeptly navigate the multifaceted terrain of leadership, collaboration, and personal growth.

Self-Reflection

i.   *When did I effectively manage my emotions in a challenging work scenario? What strategies did I use?*

ii. *In challenging situations, do I find myself reacting impulsively, or am I able to pause, assess emotions, and respond thoughtfully?*

26.

MASTERING ADAPTABILITY

Adaptability refers to the ability to adjust oneself to new situations and change one's behavior or approach in response to such situations. In the workplace, adaptability is a highly valued skill as it allows employees to be flexible and responsive to changes, challenges, and opportunities.

Developing a growth mindset is an important aspect of adaptability. This means approaching challenges and setbacks as opportunities for learning and growth, rather than fixed limitations. A growth mindset involves being open to feedback, learning from mistakes, and continuously improving oneself and one's work.

Adapting to change requires an open-minded and flexible approach to work. This implies being able to pivot when necessary, being comfortable with ambiguity, and staying calm under pressure. It also involves being proactive in seeking out new opportunities and developing new skills to stay relevant in a rapidly changing business environment.

Adaptability is the compass that navigates us through the ever-changing landscapes of career. In it lies the power to embrace new challenges, evolve with the times, and thrive in the face of constant transformation.

Examples

A few practical examples of being adaptive at workplace are:

i. **Remote ways of working during COVID-19** - Due to the Covid-19 pandemic, many companies, particularly those in the technology sector, were forced to switch to remote work. This sudden and significant change was embraced by people around the world, demonstrating their ability to adapt to new ways of working.

ii. **Return to office post-pandemic** - Based on my experience, I found it relatively more difficult to convince people to come back to office after they had become accustomed to working from home. Many employees had adjusted to the convenience of working from anywhere and transitioning back to the office posed a major challenge. This was particularly true for those who had relocated to a city different from the office location.

iii. **Change in organization structure** - At times, organizations may implement major structural changes to improve their growth, which may result in significant uncertainty within the organization. Although it may be difficult, embracing change and being more comfortable with it will ensure better professional success.

iv. **Change in company policies** - Companies may introduce new policies or modify existing ones such as leave policies or expense reimbursement policies, which may be either favorable or unfavorable for employees. It is crucial to maintain a positive outlook during such times when the changes are unfavorable, to prevent getting bogged down by negativity.

When you face varied situations at workplace, think about how you can adapt to the changing environment at while maintaining positive frame of mind. Being aware of the discomfort with change is the first step to be adaptable.

What are the benefits of being adaptive at workplace?

i. **Increased Resilience** - Being adaptive enables you to deal with uncertainty and change, which can help you bounce back quickly from setbacks and challenges.

ii. **Improved Problem-Solving** - Adaptability means being able to approach problems from different angles, using a range of solutions to find the most effective one.

iii. **Enhanced Creativity** - Adaptability involves being open to new ideas and perspectives, which can spark creativity and innovation in the workplace.

iv. **Increased Job Satisfaction** - When you are adaptive, you are better able to cope with change and uncertainty, leading to a sense of control and satisfaction in your job.

How can one be adaptive at workplace?

i. **Maintain a positive attitude** - A positive attitude can help you stay motivated and open to change.

ii. **Be open-minded** - Be willing to learn new things, accept change, consider feedback, and implement it in the way you work. This could also involve brushing your ego aside.

iii. **Stay informed** - Stay up to date with industry trends and changes within your organization. You can set automated notifications for relevant keywords on search engines to be aware of latest developments in that domain.

iv. **Continuously improve** - Seek out opportunities for professional development and skill-building. Have the mindset to be better every day in things that you do.

SUMMARY

Adaptability is about more than just adjusting to change; it is about embracing it as an opportunity for evolution. Central to this is cultivating a growth mindset, where challenges are seen as pathways to progress rather than roadblocks to success.

Adaptability is not just a skill; it is a mindset that fortifies you with increased resilience, sharper problem-solving abilities, heightened creativity, and ultimately, greater job satisfaction. Maintaining a positive attitude, staying open-minded, staying informed, and committing to continuous improvement are the cornerstones of adaptability. As you navigate the ever-changing currents of your career, remember that adaptability is your compass, guiding you to not just survive but thrive amidst the inevitable waves of change.

Self-Reflection

i. *What were some of the instances where my initial resistance to change hindered my ability to adapt, and what did I learn from those experiences?*

ii. *How have I demonstrated adaptability in response to changes or challenges in my work environment? What were the outcomes of those adaptations?*

27.

DEVELOPING A CONSULTING MINDSET

Acting like a consultant means thinking beyond the scope of one's job duties and focusing on providing value to the organization or customer. A consultant is typically hired to solve a specific problem, and they do so by using their expertise, skills, and knowledge to provide innovative and practical solutions. Similarly, developing a consulting mindset means taking a holistic approach to problem-solving and being proactive in identifying areas for improvement and offering solutions.

Some key traits of a consulting mindset include strategic thinking, strong communication skills, analytical skills, flexibility and adaptability and customer-centric focus.

In your career, be the consultant who not only solves problems, but crafts solutions that elevate.

Example

One of my team members found some insights during an analysis. She thought of follow-up analyses which required evaluating scenarios and performing simulations. She also estimated the effort involved, aligned with the manager, performed additional analyses, and came up with recommendations for the customer on what the next steps should be and which scenario was the most optimal for them. This was a clear demonstration of consulting mindset and was appreciated by the client.

What are the advantages of having consulting mindset?

i. **Improved customer experience** - By focusing on more than just providing basic solutions to customers, a consulting mindset helps to solve their underlying problems, resulting in a better customer experience. This, in turn, can lead to increased customer loyalty and retention.

ii. **Partnership with customers** - A consulting mindset allows consultants to work closely with customers, understand their unique needs and objectives, and act as long-term partners in achieving business success. This can result in increased revenue for the organization over time.

iii. **Greater efficiency** - By proactively addressing customer concerns and questions, a consulting mindset can reduce communication back-and-forth and improve overall efficiency in delivering solutions. This can result in cost savings for both the organization and the customer.

iv. **Improved problem-solving** - A consulting mindset involves a focus on understanding the root causes of problems and developing tailored solutions for customers. This approach can lead to more effective and sustainable solutions, which can in turn build trust and credibility with customers.

How can I build a consulting mindset?

Building a consulting mindset involves developing a set of skills, attitudes, and approaches that are essential for providing valuable insights and solutions to clients or within your organization. Here are a few things that you can do to develop and exhibit consulting mindset:

i. **Have the intent to be a consultant** – For some people, being a consultant comes naturally. Others can keep in mind how they can act as a consultant for their clients. This means that they will have to make a conscious attempt to not be mired in the operational work but look out for problems that their client is aiming to solve.

ii. **Listen actively and suspend judgement** - Listen objectively to what your client is sharing by putting yourself in your client's shoes. Put aside preconceived notions, assumptions, and biases that may influence your interpretation of the speaker's words. Approach the conversation with an open mind and a willingness to consider alternative viewpoints.

iii. **Ask the right questions** - Seek clarification on any aspects of the client's message that are unclear or ambiguous. Asking open-ended questions will encourage the client to elaborate further which will provide an opportunity for deeper exploration of the topic. Having good domain understanding and relevant experience will enable you to ask right question to uncover client's real challenges, pain points and processes.

iv. **Keep an open eye** – If you are already supporting the client with deliverables, stay alert for any interesting findings. Share these with the client and ask for their inputs. This shows you are curious about their business, helps you understand it better, and creates opportunities for you to add value to the client. Resist the temptation to just keep churning deliverables periodically without giving them much thought.

v. **Don't just say 'yes' to everything that your client suggests** - While being agreeable may be seen as a good quality, it need not be the case always. As a consultant, you should be mindful not to say 'yes' to everything that your client is suggesting. If you think there are better ways to solve a problem, share that with the client. Or if you disagree with client's point of view, share it with them with proper reasoning. Someone who always says 'yes' to what the client is proposing, cannot be a good 'consultant.'

vi. **Paraphrase and reflect -** Summarize and reflect on what the customer has said to ensure you have understood their message accurately. Paraphrasing shows that you are actively engaged and encourages the speaker to clarify or expand on their points if necessary.

vii. **Understanding the Current and Desired State** – The above steps i.e., listening, asking questions, paraphrasing, and reflecting will help you understand the client's current situation (where they are currently and what problem they are looking to solve) and desired situation (where they want to be). Occasionally, clients may struggle to envision their desired state of success or improvement. In such instances, it falls upon you to offer suggestions based on your expertise. Collaborating internally and drawing upon the experiences of others within your organization can also enrich your recommendations to the client.

viii. **Identifying How to Get There** - Once you have understood the current and desired states, the next step is crafting the roadmap. Propose solutions and strategies that serve as the bridge between the two.

This involves not only addressing immediate concerns but also offering a sustainable path for continuous improvement. Your role as a consultant is not just to solve problems but to guide the client on a journey of growth.

Focus on delivering practical, actionable solutions that address the client's needs and objectives. Present recommendations that are feasible, cost-effective, and scalable, considering the client's resources, timeline, and constraints. This may involve data analysis, scenario simulation, benchmarking studies, change management etc. depending on the client's situation.

ix. **Provide scenarios and options to client** – In your discussions with the client through the consulting project, make them feel a part of the consulting engagement. The recommendation that you have for them at the end of the project should not be a surprize for them. And instead of just asking the client to do what you have recommended, present them with a couple of options and let them choose. This empowers them to take a decision on what they think would work best.

x. **Speak the client's language** - Communicate in terms that resonate with the client, using industry-specific terminology and avoiding jargon that may be unfamiliar to them. Tailor your messages to their level of understanding and organizational culture to ensure clarity and alignment.

xi. **Add Value**: Offer insights, expertise, and perspectives that add tangible value to the client's business. Provide innovative ideas, best practices, and industry benchmarks that demonstrate your thought leadership and contribute to their success.

Note: While this chapter delves into cultivating a consulting mindset, its aim is not to transform employees into traditional consultants tasked with addressing specific issues within a consulting project. Rather, the emphasis lies in empowering employees to adopt a consultative approach in their daily roles, thereby enhancing value delivery for customers. Instead of solely delivering mandated reports, the focus shifts towards comprehending clients' challenges and actively contributing to their resolution. Embracing such opportunities not only allows employees to serve as ambassadors for their organization but also fosters a sense of fulfilment in addressing client needs, potentially elevating client relationships to new heights.

SUMMARY

In conclusion, adopting a consulting mindset is not just about solving problems; it is about crafting solutions that elevate. By thinking beyond the scope of your job duties and focusing on providing value to your organization or customers, you can improve the overall customer experience, forge strong partnerships, increase efficiency, and enhance problem-solving capabilities. Building a consulting mindset involves actively listening, asking the right questions, and keeping an open eye for opportunities to add value. It is about understanding the current and desired states, crafting practical solutions, and speaking the client's language to ensure clarity and alignment. By embracing these principles, you can contribute to the success of your organization and foster meaningful client relationships, ultimately driving growth and innovation. Remember, the goal is not only to transform into a traditional consultant, but rather to empower yourself to adopt a consultative approach in your daily role, thereby enhancing value delivery for your customers.

Self-Reflection

i.   *How well do I delve into the underlying complexities of the issues rather than focusing solely on surface-level problems?*

ii. *In what ways do I position myself as a trusted advisor, guiding clients toward ongoing success rather than offering quick fixes?*

28.

POLITICAL SAVVINESS

As you progress in your career, you may encounter situations that are not straightforward, with answers that are not as simple as saying "yes" or "no," or labeling them as "right" or "wrong." You may find yourself in situations where two parties have conflicting goals, or where one party is attempting to obstruct another party's success. In such cases, you must be politically astute and carefully navigate the situation to avoid harming either party while still achieving a mutually beneficial outcome.

Political savviness is the strategic compass in professional waters empowering impactful moves while maintaining delicate relationships in the organization.

Being politically savvy in work context refers to the ability to understand and navigate the complex social dynamics that exist within an organization. This includes having a keen awareness of the power structures, for example, who has more power or power to make decisions, social norms, and unwritten rules that govern the behavior of individuals and groups in the office. It also means being able to build and maintain positive relationships with colleagues and stakeholders, while also avoiding potentially damaging conflicts or miscommunications. It involves communicating effectively with a diverse range of individuals and adapting your communication style to different situations and personalities.

Example

When COVID-19 just struck, in one of the multi-country projects we had to define the best way track interactions with our organization's customers. At that time, face-to-face interactions between company's sales representatives and its customers were severely impacted. Therefore, customer interactions were only happening virtually via video calls and phone calls. To calculate one of the KPIs (key performance indicators) in a report, one country suggested that phone calls should be considered for calculating the KPI, while another suggested that it was too easy to make a phone call to customers and anyone could do it without much effort, and hence it should not be considered. There were arguments from both sides in favour of their viewpoint. As I sensed that the discussion was starting to get heated, instead of taking sides, I proposed that we can create two KPIs - one would include phone calls and the other would not. This would also provide insight into the proportion of interactions occurring via channels other than phone calls, compared to those occurring through phone calls. Both countries agreed to it. Through patient mediation and skilful negotiation, countries reached a mutually acceptable solution, allowing the project to move forward without escalating tensions or jeopardizing relationships.

What are the advantages of being politically savvy?

i. **Better communication** - Political agility requires an increased awareness of social cues and the ability to adapt communication styles to different individuals and situations. This can lead to more effective communication and better relationships with colleagues, superiors, and customers.

ii. **Increased influence** - Politically agile individuals are often able to build strong networks and alliances, which can help them achieve their goals more effectively. They can also navigate organizational hierarchies more successfully and influence decision-making processes.

iii. **Career advancement** - Being politically agile can be a crucial factor in career advancement, as it enables individuals to build a positive reputation, gain recognition for their achievements, and secure opportunities for growth and development.

iv. **Enhanced problem-solving** - Political agility requires individuals to be open to different perspectives and ideas, and to find creative solutions to complex problems. This can lead to more innovative and effective problem-solving and can help organizations to remain competitive and adaptable.

v. **Improved organizational culture** - Politically agile individuals can contribute to a more positive organizational culture by promoting cooperation, trust, and mutual respect. This can create a more supportive and productive environment for everyone.

How can I be politically agile?

i. **Build relationships** - Take the time to get to know your colleagues and understand their perspectives. Build a network of allies and supporters who can help you navigate complex situations.

ii. **Listen actively** - Listen carefully to what others are saying and try to understand their motivations and concerns. This can help you anticipate potential issues and identify areas of common ground.

iii. **Communicate effectively** - Be clear and concise in your communication, and tailor your message to your audience. Use diplomacy and tact when dealing with difficult situations or conflicts.

iv. **Manage conflict** - Learn how to manage conflict effectively, using negotiation and mediation skills where necessary. Avoid taking sides or becoming involved in office politics.

v. **Stay informed** - Stay up to date with the latest industry news and trends and be aware of any internal or external factors that may impact your organization.

vi. **Be adaptable** - Be flexible and willing to adapt to changing circumstances or new information. Avoid being rigid or inflexible in your approach.

Distinguishing between political agility and negative office politics is crucial. Political agility involves effectively navigating organizational dynamics to achieve goals and positively influence outcomes, while negative office politics entail manipulative behaviors that undermine trust and collaboration. Political agility entails building relationships, understanding power dynamics, and ethically leveraging influence to drive positive outcomes. In contrast, negative office politics involve behaviors like manipulation, gossiping, and seeking personal gain at others' expense, which erode trust and hinder productivity.

In essence, while political agility focuses on constructive engagement and strategic manoeuvring to navigate organizational complexities, negative office politics revolve around selfish motives and destructive behaviors that undermine the overall health and effectiveness of the workplace. As you strive to develop political agility, it is essential to cultivate a mindset of integrity, empathy, and collaboration, ensuring that your actions contribute positively to the organization's success while avoiding the pitfalls of negative office politics.

SUMMARY

Mastering political savviness in your career journey is like wielding a strategic compass in professional waters, navigating relationships while making impactful moves. It is about understanding workplace dynamics and effectively communicating, building relationships, and managing conflicts.

The benefits include improved communication, increased influence, career advancement, enhanced problem-solving, and contributing to a positive organizational culture. Remember, political agility involves constructive engagement, steering clear of negative office politics, and acting with integrity, empathy, and collaboration to propel both your career and the organization toward success.

Self-Reflection

i. *In what ways do I actively seek to understand the motivations, interests, and alliances of key individuals in my workplace?*

ii. *What approaches have I employed to build positive relationships with colleagues or superiors?*

29.

THINKING STRATEGICALLY

Strategic thinking is about deciding today where we want the organization to be tomorrow, and how will we get there. In other words, it is about *'where to play'* and *'how to win.'* Once the organization defines its strategy, it needs to define tactics to get where it wants to be. Strategic thinking focuses on finding and developing unique opportunities to create value for the organisation. It means thinking ahead and planning to achieve success rather than simply reacting to the competition or making short-term fixes that may not be sustainable in the long run. While strategic thinking helps define what the organization will focus on, it also gives clarity on what the organization will *not* focus on.

When you are in the initial stages of your career, you are focused more on executing tasks, delivering to customers, issue resolution, making sure you deliver to the customer with quality, on time. As you move forward in your career, one of the most important skills that is required is strategic thinking. This means defining what kind of projects your organization might take or reject. Any organization will have limited resources and has to achieve its objectives using those limited resources. A strategy will help prioritize what kind of products or services the organization should focus on to create maximum value for its shareholders given the limited resources.

Strategic thinking is the blueprint of success, the compass of innovation, and the driving force behind navigating challenges with foresight.

Example

For one of our customers, which was culturally quite different from the western world, we had to penetrate and get more business. The typical approach of showcasing our capabilities and project experience wasn't working. Hence, we had to think strategically on how we could approach that country.

Where to play - We computed the total addressable market for the customer, identified whitespaces, and conducted a thorough analysis of the company's strengths, weaknesses, opportunities, and threats (SWOT analysis). Based on this, we were able to identify the potential opportunities for us to grow. *How to win* - Rather than working in silos to get more business, we started collaborating more with the information technology (IT), procurement and other teams who were already supporting that country. We also thought of the capabilities required to be better positioned to support the country, for example, having a physical presence in the market and the language skills, as the country was non-English speaking. This would have been difficult if we did not take a structured strategic thinking approach.

Why do you need to be strategic?

i.   **Meet expectations** - Being strategic will no longer be an option as you progress in your career. While in early stages, you will be able to sail though without being strategic, it will become a bottleneck for your growth if you don't start thinking strategically or long term.

ii. **Improved decision making** - Strategic thinking involves considering multiple options and weighing the pros and cons of each and choosing one that aligns best with organizational strategic direction, which can result in better decision making.

iii. **Better resource allocation** - Strategic thinking helps in identifying and prioritizing key areas to allocate resources while also helping with areas where resources should not be focused, resulting in a more effective and efficient utilization of resources.

iv. **Flexibility** - Strategic thinking involves considering multiple scenarios and being able to adapt to changing circumstances, which can help organizations be more resilient and able to navigate unexpected challenges.

v. **Competitive advantage** - Strategic thinking helps to identify opportunities and threats in the market, which can lead to a competitive advantage over other organizations.

How can you hone your strategic thinking skills?

Most likely, no one will train you to be a 'strategic thinker.' While you may get exposed to some trainings sessions around strategy, most learning will come from hands-on experience. Ask your manager proactively to delegate some tasks to you which involve thinking strategically. You can share a first draft of your solution or approach with your manager and they can refine it as needed or guide you to refine it. If you can see what, how and why they refine something, it will be immense value addition to you. Repeated exposure to such tasks will get you an experience of how to think strategically which you will gradually start demonstrating independently. Also, have an open discussion with your mentor, who need not necessarily be your manager, on how you can enhance your strategic thinking skill. Other ways to develop strategic thinking are:

i. **Read and study** - Reading books and articles on strategy and business can help you develop your knowledge of the subject and provide you with ideas and concepts to apply in your work.

ii. **Attend training programs** - Many organizations offer training programs in strategic thinking, which can help you learn new techniques and approaches.

iii. **Seek mentorship** - Finding a mentor who is skilled in strategic thinking can be an invaluable resource for developing your own skills.

iv. **Practice** - Practice strategic thinking in your own work by identifying long-term goals, anticipating challenges, and developing plans to achieve those goals.

v. **Engage in critical thinking** - Critical thinking involves analyzing problems and developing solutions, which is a key aspect of strategic thinking. Engage in critical thinking exercises regularly to hone your skills.

vi. **Collaborate** - Working with others can help you develop your strategic thinking skills by exposing you to different perspectives and approaches. Seek out opportunities to collaborate with others on strategic projects.

SUMMARY

Strategic thinking is the cornerstone of success in the professional world. It is the mindset that propels you beyond mere task execution to envisioning and navigating the future of your organization. As you progress in your career, this skill becomes indispensable, offering clarity, better decision-making, resource optimization, and adaptability. To hone your strategic prowess, immerse yourself in strategic projects, seek mentorship, and continuously learn through reading, training, and critical thinking. Embrace collaboration and actively challenge yourself to think innovatively. Strategic thinking is not just a destination;

it is a journey of continual growth and adaptation, ensuring your relevance and success in a dynamic landscape.

Self-Reflection

i. *How often do I step back from day-to-day tasks to assess the broader goals and objectives of my team or organization?*

ii. *Are there specific mentors or role models in the organization known for their strategic acumen, and how can I learn from their approaches?*

30.

NURTURING A POSITIVE MINDSET

A positive mindset can make all the difference in achieving success in both personal and professional life. A positive mindset is a mental state that enables individuals to focus on the positive aspects of life and approach challenges with a can-do attitude. It is not about ignoring the negative aspects of life, but rather, focusing on the solutions and possibilities that exist.

Positivity is the energy that fuels achievement. Let optimism be the driving force in your career journey.

To thrive in your career, it is important to have a positive outlook. During the early stages of your career, you may face numerous challenges that can trigger negative thoughts. However, it is important to understand that this is a natural human response that evolved from the need to survive in ancient times when people had to protect themselves from wild animals. To overcome this natural tendency towards negativity, you must actively work towards cultivating and maintaining a positive mindset. It can be easy to become trapped in a negative mindset, so you must make a conscious effort to break free from this cycle.

Example

During a project, a crisis situation emerged when a critical customer was unhappy and was on the verge of switching to a competitor. With the support of leadership, we convinced the customer to give us three months to turn the situation around. The entire team was under pressure to deliver on time with high quality, as any mistake during this period could have cost us customer churn. I encouraged my team to view it as a learning opportunity and to come out of it successfully with a valuable experience. We hired new team members, which led to some conflicts. However, I assured the team that conflicts are natural in a new team and will settle with time. By maintaining composure and taking the pressure off the team, we were able to meet our quality targets. The customer was happy with the outcomes of the turnaround situation and continued the engagement with us. Instead of blaming external factors, I took the approach of focusing on the positive and maintaining a calm and supportive environment for the team which led us to achieve positive outcomes.

A negative approach to handling this situation would have been to react with panic and blame, rather than remaining calm and supportive. Instead of reassuring the team and encouraging them to view the situation as a learning opportunity, I could have expressed frustration or placed blame on team members for conflicts. This approach could have increased tension within the team and hindered their ability to work effectively under pressure. Additionally, if I had not demonstrated resilience and effectively managed the crisis and instead succumbed to the pressure, it could have resulted in losing the customer, leading to negative consequences for the team and the organization.

What are the advantages of having a positive mindset?

i. **It's contagious** - Thinking and talking positively with others makes them do the same. If you see someone talking negatively, try changing their thoughts with your positivity. This way you can spread positivity around, in the workplace.

ii. **Increases productivity** - When you have a positive mindset, you are more likely to be focused, energized, and motivated to achieve your goals. This, in turn, leads to increased productivity.

iii. **Enhances resilience** - In the workplace, you are likely to face various challenges and setbacks. Having a positive mindset helps you bounce back from these setbacks quickly and remain optimistic about the future.

iv. **Reduces stress** - Stress can harm your health, mood, and productivity. A positive mindset can help reduce stress levels and improve your overall well-being.

How can you develop and maintain a positive mindset?

Here are a few ways you can develop and sustain a positive mindset, though it may not really be as easy as it sounds:

i. **Challenges are natural** - Recognize that challenges and adversities are inherent aspects of life. Every distinguished leader and notable figure have faced challenges in their journey, and we are no exception.

ii. **Put yourself in others' shoes** - If you struggle to comprehend why someone is acting a certain way, attempt to empathize by putting yourself in their shoes. Consider the potential constraints or pressures that may be influencing their decisions, which you find challenging to comprehend.

iii. **Be aware** - If you are aware that you are gravitating towards a negative mindset, you can stop yourself from getting there. 'Distract' yourself to redirect yourself to the positive zone.

iv. **Practice gratitude** - Start your day by expressing gratitude for the things you have. This will help you focus on the positive aspects of your life and appreciate what you have.

v. **Focus on solutions, not problems** - Instead of focusing on the problems, focus on finding solutions to those problems. This will help you maintain a positive outlook and avoid feeling overwhelmed.

vi. **Have a positive company** - Surrounding yourself with positive and supportive colleagues can help boost your morale and keep you motivated.

vii. **Embrace feedback** - You will get a lot of feedback, comments, and suggestions for whatever you do. This does not mean what you originally did was not good. Take the inputs from others positively as an opportunity to learn and grow.

viii. **Celebrate small wins** - Celebrate small achievements and progress towards your goals. This will help you stay motivated and maintain a positive mindset.

ix. **Practice mindfulness** - Practicing mindfulness can help you stay present and avoid getting bogged down by negative thoughts. Try taking a few minutes every day to meditate or practice deep breathing exercises.

Note: Occasionally, someone we admire may say something that hurts us. In these times, remember that they are human and did not intend to hurt us. They may have spoken those words out of their own distress. As humans, we sometimes say unkind things when we are upset. Therefore, do not take such comments to heart if they occur infrequently. However, be cautious of repeated abusive behavior. If you notice a repeated pattern, it is best to distance yourself from such a person.

SUMMARY

In summary, nurturing a positive mindset is not just a desirable trait; it is a crucial element for success in your personal and professional life. It is about embracing challenges as opportunities, maintaining composure under pressure, and focusing on solutions rather than dwelling on problems. By cultivating gratitude, empathy, and resilience, you can develop a mindset that not only enhances your own well-being but also positively influences those around you. Remember, positivity is contagious, and by actively practicing it, you can create a ripple effect of optimism in your workplace and beyond. So, as you embark on your career journey, let positivity be your guiding light, fueling your aspirations and propelling you towards your goals.

Self-Reflection

i. *When did I successfully turn a negative situation into an opportunity? What mindset shift did I experience, and how did it influence the outcome?*

ii. *How can I cultivate a more positive mindset in my daily work life?*

31.

DECODING NETWORKING

Professional networking is the practice of building and maintaining contacts and relationships with colleagues, managers, customers, and other stakeholders in one's professional sphere. It involves strategically connecting with others to exchange information, share ideas, seek advice, and create opportunities for collaboration and advancement. The goal of networking is to create a supportive network of peers and contacts that help foster career success.

Example

One of the individuals on my team was exceptional in networking. Despite the hesitation that many people have in approaching unknown individuals, this team member was proactive in reaching out to people when required. Additionally, once the specific need was fulfilled, this team member continued to stay in touch with those individuals, including senior leaders, through periodic connects to maintain the relationship. This resulted in the individual building their own network which not only benefitted them, but which I as a manager could also leverage.

In the network of relationships, build bridges that withstand the tests of time. Connect, nurture, and thrive.

What are the advantages of networking?

i. **Enhanced visibility** – Engaging in professional networking boosts your visibility and recognition among potential employers and industry contacts. This can make you more attractive to prospective employers when it comes to new job opportunities.

ii. **Stronger network** - Professional networking is an effective way to find mentors and establish meaningful relationships with other professionals. It is a great way to stay connected with people in your field and build relationships that may lead to exciting opportunities.

iii. **Stay informed** - Networking keeps you informed about new trends, concepts, and information within your industry. It is a great way to stay up to date on industry knowledge, connect with professionals in various roles, and access job opportunities you may not have considered.

iv. **Learning & development** - Professional networking offers the opportunity to learn from different professionals, from both inside and outside of your industry. Whether you are seeking advice or listening to experiences of others, it is a great chance to learn from those with more experience or expertise in specific areas.

How can I network at my office or in the industry?

i. **Attend events** - Events, such as conferences, networking meetups, and corporate sports events, are great opportunities to meet new people and learn about new ideas and trends in your industry. Taking part in these events can help to expand your network, provide new perspectives, and help to foster relationships with key contacts.

ii. **Volunteer in events** - Besides just participating, you can support organizing events and activities which involve working with unknown people. Through this, you will be able to meet new people and they will be able to see your expertise and leadership.

iii. **Reach meetings before time** - Reaching meetings a few minutes before time will enable you to connect with others who are before time for the same meeting. You could use that time to introduce yourself to them and get to know them better.

iv. **Be willing to help** - Being willing to help, even if it sometimes means that you have to put in extra effort to help someone. This can go a long way in building and maintaining relationships. People usually remember the support that you provided them and are more than willing to help later.

v. **Nurture relationships** - Networking is not just about building connections. You need to nurture relationships to maintain them. Stay connected with your contacts and follow up with them after meeting. Following some of the best practices in this book on various elements can also help you maintain relationships with your stakeholders. And sometimes, in a discussion with others, be willing to lose an argument, to win over them.

vi. **Share relevant content** - Adding value to your professional network is essential to staying connected and growing your connections. Share your knowledge and experiences through blog posts and videos, comment on posts, and help engage in conversations within your networks.

SUMMARY

The essence of networking is not just about exchanging business cards; it is about building enduring bridges. From being proactive in reaching out to nurturing connections over time, you've discovered its power. By attending events, volunteering, arriving early, helping, and sharing relevant content, you can increase visibility, strengthen your network, stay informed, and continue to grow professionally. Every connection made is an opportunity for collaboration and growth. Connect, nurture, and thrive in your professional network - it is the cornerstone of your career success.

Self-Reflection

i. *How diverse is my current professional network in terms of roles, industries, and expertise?*

ii. *How do I initiate conversations and build connections with new people, both inside and outside my organization?*

32.

ISSUE HANDLING AND RESILIENCE

Issue handling refers to the process of identifying, assessing, and resolving issues or problems that happen during the course of work. It involves the ability to effectively deal with issues that impact the quality of a project. For the purpose of this book, we will limit the scope to consider issues only in products and services that adversely impact the customer experience.

Resilience is the armor that shields your career. Face challenges with strength, and let setbacks be stepping stones.

The goal of issue handling is to address problems in a timely and effective manner, thereby preventing them from escalating into more significant issues that can adversely affect the customer experience. Many aspects discussed in this book can help with issue management such as proactivity, being action oriented to resolve the issue, and being open ended for the feedback from manager or customers.

The topic of issue handling can be considered as a part of the broad topic of quality. We will discuss it in this chapter at a broad level without getting into specifics.

Issue handling starts with recognizing and accepting that an issue has happened. Many a times, individuals may not openly discuss issues. They may also brush issues discovered after the delivery of products or services to customers under the carpet.

Upon identifying an error in your work, the first step will be to notify your manager and engage in a discussion about subsequent steps. Work to understand the severity and impact of the issue. Based on my experience, it is advisable to proactively inform the customer of the issue before they uncover it, preventing them from perceiving it as an oversight on your part if they discovered it themselves. However, it is best to align with your manager on the approach of handling the issue and communicating to your customer, as this could vary from organization to organization depending on the culture and prevalent practices.

If you are talking to the customer, apologize genuinely for the issue and the inconvenience caused. Customers may react to it in different intensities. What will be important is, if they are angry or frustrated, let them vent out their anger or frustration. Give it a patient hearing without trying to justify why the mistake happened. Your customers may not sound logical at this point. But most likely, their knee-jerk reaction will subside over time. You can walk them through the root cause analysis of why the mistake happened. Next, propose to them the corrective actions and preventive actions (CAPA) that you have already taken or plan to take to ensure that the same or similar issue does not recur. This will typically include timelines as well and actions should be completed before the next delivery.

Ensure that there are no errors in subsequent deliveries, as that will be detrimental to the trust built over the years. Have a connect with stakeholders to update them when all actions have been completed. Also, document all of these in slides or email to ensure there is no scope for misunderstanding. Being fast paced and action-oriented in this entire process will help give confidence to the customer that you are taking the issue seriously and working extra hard to prevent them in the future. Capture lessons learnt from these issues and share with wider group so that the entire organization leans from it.

While issue handling here refers mostly to customer related issues, issues can occur within a team or across teams. Then there may be technical issues or unforeseen situations like the pandemic. Whatever the situation be, as a leader, how you handle it will determine the level of trust and confidence that you build with your teams.

It is important to acknowledge that issues can be either real or perceptual. Perceptual issues refer to situations where there are no actual problems, but people believe that things are not going well. This can be the case with customers or even with your own leaders. In such situations, it is important to recognize that there is a negative perception, objectively evaluate the situation, and proactively use data and effective communication to dispel any incorrect beliefs.

Example

One of my customers once expressed dissatisfaction with my team's responsiveness over last few months. However, my team disagreed with the customer's perception. To address the issue, I examined the past three months of customer emails and checked whether the team had responded according to the agreed timelines. Upon reviewing the data, it became evident that the delay was only a matter of perception and not reality. I shared this data with the customer, who agreed with my assessment. I also informed the customer that if they encountered any issues, they could bring them to my attention in almost real-time rather than waiting for a complete quarter for us to share the feedback survey or when I would explicitly reach out to them for feedback. By providing early feedback, we could promptly address any issues and provide the customer with a better experience. This approach promotes joint accountability, and prompt addressing of any potential issues or risks.

What are the advantages of effective issue handling?

i. **Improved productivity** - By addressing issues quickly, employees can spend less time dealing with problems and more time being productive and focusing on their tasks.

ii. **Better team morale** - When issues are handled quickly and effectively, it can boost team morale and create a positive work environment. Employees feel supported and valued by their employer.

iii. **Reduced stress** - When employees feel that issues are being taken seriously and addressed promptly, it can reduce their stress levels and improve their overall well-being.

iv. **Improved customer satisfaction** - Addressing issues promptly can improve customer satisfaction and retention, as customers feel their concerns are being heard and taken seriously.

How can you go about issue handling?

i. **Identify the issue** - The first step is to identify the issue and clearly define what the problem is. You would need to understand and fix the root cause and not the symptoms (e.g., treating fever (symptom) vs. bacterial infection (root cause)).

ii. **Gather data** - Collect relevant information related to the issue, such as the people involved, timing, impact, and any other pertinent details.

iii. **Analyze data** - Evaluate the information and try to understand the root cause of the issue. Determine the factors that contribute to the problem.

iv. **Plan for solution** - Based on the analysis, develop a plan to address the issue. Determine the steps that need to be taken to resolve the issue and identify the resources that will be needed.

v. **Implement solutions** - Implement the plan and take necessary actions to address the issue. This may involve having difficult conversations, making changes to processes, or taking other corrective actions.

vi. **Monitor progress** - Keep track of progress in resolving the issue. Monitor the situation and make any necessary adjustments to the plan.

vii. **Evaluate outcome** - Once the issue is resolved, evaluate the outcome to ensure that the problem is fully addressed, and measures are in place to prevent it from happening again in the future.

viii. **Be Proactive** - To avoid future issues, use approaches to proactively identify failure points and fix them. The quality in-charge in your organization should be able to help with this.

Note: Ignoring issues or delaying their resolution at work can result in bigger problems down the line. It could also lead to loss of business for the organization if the customer decides to work with someone else instead of your organization. Prompt issue handling can prevent issues from escalating and becoming more difficult to resolve.

As a leader what is your approach of handling issues? Do you pass on the stress and pressure of being in a crisis situation to your team members? Or do you cushion them by absorbing stress and pressure yourself so that they can focus more on resolving the issue? Your team will remember you for how you made them *feel* while handling the situation.

SUMMARY

Issue handling and resilience are indispensable elements in navigating the complex terrain of your career. Embrace the challenges with fortitude and consider them as opportunities in disguise. Whether it is addressing customer concerns or internal team issues, your ability to swiftly identify, assess, and resolve problems is pivotal. Remember, resilience is not just about bouncing back; it is about bouncing forward. Each setback is a chance to learn, grow, and strengthen your professional armor. By approaching issues with proactive vigor, open communication, and a commitment to continuous improvement, you not only safeguard your career but also foster a culture of trust, accountability, and excellence. So, equip yourself with resilience, and let every challenge be a testament to your unwavering determination and capability.

Self-Reflection

i.   *How did my manager handle a major issue in a deliverable or a client escalation? What are my leanings from that instance? What would I have done differently?*

ii. *How do I typically respond to unexpected challenges or setbacks in my work?*

33.

UNVEILING THE ART OF LEADERSHIP

Leadership is very elaborate topic and can be known by many names like 'Team Leadership,' 'Organizational Leadership' or 'Business Leadership.' There is a lot of literature on the internet, plethora of courses on e-learning platforms, and a gamut of books available to read on these topics. Considering the importance of this topic in one's career, I will briefly highlight a few elements that budding leaders can keep in mind:

i. **Vision** - A leader should not just have a clear vision but should also be able to communicate it effectively to their team.

ii. **Integrity** - A leader should be honest, trustworthy, and act with integrity in all their dealings.

iii. **Communication** - A leader should be an effective communicator, able to listen actively, provide clear instructions, and give feedback constructively.

iv. **Empathy** - A leader should be able to understand and empathize with their team members' needs and feelings.

v. **Decisiveness** - A leader should be able to make quick and effective decisions, even in high-pressure situations.

vi. **Adaptability** - A leader should be able to adapt to changing circumstances and be open to new ideas and approaches.

vii. **Accountability** - A leader should take responsibility for their actions and decisions, as well as those of their team.

viii. **Approachability** - A leader should be open and approachable by their team members.

ix. **Business acumen** - A leader should know how business works, know industry trends and competition and be aware of how strategies and tactics work.

x. **Confidence** - A leader should have confidence in their abilities and decisions, but also be open to feedback and willing to learn from mistakes.

xi. **Creativity** - A leader should be able to think creatively and come up with innovative solutions to problems.

xii. **Resilience** - Leaders who can bounce back from setbacks and persevere through challenges demonstrate resilience, which is an important trait for achieving long-term success.

xiii. **Humour** - A good leader should have a decent sense of humour to make the environment light when needed.

xiv. **Listener** - A good leader should focus more on listening than speaking to their associates.

A few additional aspects that leaders can keep in mind when managing people are as follows:

i. **Motivation** - A good manager knows how to motivate their team. This can be done in many ways including recognition and rewards, providing opportunities for growth and development, and ensuring that everyone feels valued and appreciated.

ii. **Empowering others** - A good people leader trusts their team and empowers them to take ownership of their work. They provide the necessary guidance and support, but ultimately allow their team members to make decisions and take action.

iii. **Delegation** - Delegating tasks to team members can be a great way to empower them and help them develop new skills. It is important to delegate tasks that match the team member's skill set and to provide them with the necessary support and resources.

iv. **Openness and transparency** - A good people leader is honest, transparent, and open with their team. They share information freely, communicate their vision and goals clearly, and actively seek input and feedback from their team.

v. **Conflict resolution** - Conflicts are inevitable in any workplace, but a good manager knows how to handle them effectively. This involves actively listening to both sides, finding common ground, and producing a mutually beneficial solution.

vi. **Ability to coach and mentor** - People leaders should be able to coach and mentor their team members to help them grow and develop their skills. This includes providing guidance and feedback, identifying opportunities for growth and development, and supporting their team members in achieving their goals. A good leader should create their succession plan.

vii. **Emotional intelligence** - A people leader with high emotional intelligence can understand and manage their own emotions, as well as the emotions of others. They are able to create a positive and supportive work environment and can navigate conflicts and challenges with empathy and compassion.

Leadership is not about commanding authority, but about inspiring others to unleash their potential and achieve greatness.

Note: As you work alongside your managers, you may admire certain qualities they possess while disliking others. However, it is important not to simply imitate your manager's behavior when you become a leader. Instead, consider which qualities you want to imbibe from them and continue to exhibit those behaviors. Conversely, avoid emulating behaviors that you did not appreciate in them. By recognizing the desirable and undesirable behaviors, you can enhance your leadership skills and become more effective in leading people and teams.

SUMMARY

As you embark on your journey towards leadership, remember that it is not just about wielding authority but about igniting the potential within others to achieve greatness. Learn from the diverse array of leaders you encounter, cherry-picking the qualities you admire while consciously avoiding those with which you do not resonate. By honing your unique blend of leadership traits and continuously refining your approach, you can inspire and empower those around you to soar to new heights, fostering a culture of collaboration, growth, and achievement.

Self-Reflection

i.   *What are the qualities that I admire in my current or previous managers?*

ii. *As I become a manager or a leader myself, what would I like to do differently compared to my managers/leaders?*

34.

CRAFTING YOUR PROFESSIONAL PERSONA

Today, the 'professional success' paradigm has shifted beyond the traditional emphasis on day-to-day performance. While proficiency in your role remains fundamental, understanding and embracing aspects beyond performance are pivotal for unlocking the full spectrum of career opportunities. Therefore, it becomes imperative to explore the essential aspects to consider beyond performance and delve into the reasons behind their significance.

The P.I.E. Theory of Success, coined by Harvey J. Coleman, sheds light on the multifaceted aspects that contribute to career advancement. This framework provides a practical approach to thinking beyond performance and focusing on other critical factors that lead to success in the workplace.

The "P" in PIE represents performance, indicating how well an individual executes the responsibilities outlined in their role. Despite the common belief that impressive performance leads to promotions, it holds a mere 10 percent weight in the decision-making process. This seemingly low significance stems from the fact that meeting job expectations is already assumed. Therefore, to stand out in terms of performance, individuals must not only fulfil their duties but also demonstrate exceptional contributions that go beyond the expected.

Moving on to the "I" in PIE, which stands for image, it denotes the personal brand or reputation one holds within the organization. This aspect contributes 30 percent towards promotion considerations, highlighting its significance. An individual's image is formed by the perceptions others have of them, shaped by numerous factors such as communication style, demeanor, and approach to work. Managing one's image involves presenting oneself in a manner that fosters trust and credibility, as these qualities are pivotal for gaining support and influence within the organizational hierarchy.

Lastly, the "E" in PIE, exposure, commands the most weight at 60 percent when it comes to promotion evaluations. Exposure refers to the visibility an individual and their achievements have among key decision-makers within the organization. It is not merely about being well-known but rather being seen succeeding and making impactful contributions that resonate with senior leadership. Building a broad network of advocates, including mentors and sponsors, is crucial for increasing exposure and gaining recognition for one's capabilities. Ultimately, high exposure enhances familiarity and trust among decision-makers, positioning individuals favorably for career advancement opportunities.

Reflecting on the promotion discussions for employees that I have been a part of, I can say that leaders often prioritize exposure and image when identifying future leaders. While excellent performance is a prerequisite for any candidate who is eligible for promotion, being known, recognized, and having a positive image contribute significantly to a favorable promotion decision for an individual. The reasoning behind this approach lies in the understanding that future leaders in the organization must be more than proficient - they must inspire, collaborate, and positively impact their surroundings. Managers seek individuals who embody the values and culture of the organization, and exposure and image play key roles in highlighting these qualities.

It is vital to recognize that elements beyond performance are not merely additional considerations but integral components of a holistic career strategy. While organizations can provide opportunities for exposure and managers can offer guidance, personal accountability is paramount. Proactive career development involves actively managing your image, seeking opportunities for strategic exposure, and adapting to the changing professional landscape. By embracing personal branding, strategic visibility, adaptability, and understanding managerial perspectives, you can transcend the conventional boundaries of success and chart a course for enduring and fulfilling careers.

By focusing on performance, image, and exposure, you can build a strong foundation for a successful career and achieve your goals in the long term.

In the pursuit of excellence, transcend mere performance. Think beyond, aspire for greatness, and let your career be legendary.

SUMMARY

In conclusion, crafting your professional persona extends far beyond mere performance. As highlighted by the P.I.E. Theory of Success, your image and exposure are equally vital. While proficiency in your role is essential, managing your reputation and seeking strategic visibility are key factors in career advancement. By proactively shaping your personal brand, fostering trust, and showcasing your contributions, you lay the foundation for enduring success. Embrace these principles, aspire for greatness, and let your career journey be nothing short of legendary.

Self-Reflection

i. *What are the steps I take to improve the 'image' and 'exposure' aspects of the P.I.E. framework?*

ii. *What would I like to do differently to enhance my 'image' and 'exposure'?*

35.

LEVERAGING GENAI FOR CAREER ADVANCEMENT

Generative AI, or GenAI, is a transformative technology that has democratized usage of artificial intelligence. Leaders across industries and organizations are eager to utilize GenAI to create an impact by transforming their businesses through enhanced creativity, efficiency, personalization, and strategic renewal. Let us briefly explore how GenAI can be beneficial from a career perspective.

Given the multitude of tasks GenAI can perform, it may seem threatening to many of us, raising concerns about whether machines will replace our jobs. I attended a healthcare conference in a prestigious management institute. At that conference, a session on 'AI in Healthcare' featured a question from a doctor: "Will AI take our jobs?" The speaker's response was compelling: "AI will not take your jobs. Doctors using AI will take jobs from doctors not using AI." This statement holds true not just for doctors but for any profession. Those who leverage AI will outpace those who do not, making it crucial to stay updated on technological advancements in GenAI and leveraging them to our advantage.

While the potential applications of AI vary by industry, some common use cases include:

i. **Idea generation** – GenAI can help generate initial ideas on any topic or problem at hand, which you can then refine or expand upon.

ii. **Idea augmentation** – If you already have ideas, GenAI can enhance them by suggesting improvements or adding new dimensions to those ideas.

iii. **Idea validation, selection, and feedback** – GenAI provides an objective perspective on ideas, acting as a sounding board to help select the best ones and offer feedback.

iv. **Secondary research** – AI tools can expedite secondary research on any topic by consolidating information from multiple sources on the internet and providing relevant links to those sources. These searches are much more efficient compared to 'traditional' ways of performing internet research.

v. **Writing** – AI writing assistants can draft content such as articles, emails, or presentations, which you can then refine as per your requirement.

vi. **Reviewing content** – GenAI can help review email drafts created by you. For example, checking if the content and tone of the email is appropriate or not and how you can make the message concise and effective.

vii. **Coaching** – GenAI can serve as a career coach, offering suggestions for workplace challenges. GenAI is not a replacement for an experienced professional or a professional coach. Therefore, it is important to critically assess these suggestions for practicality before implementation.

viii. **Generating code** – Instead of writing codes from scratch, GenAI can generate code in various programming languages which you can tweak for your purpose, boosting productivity significantly. It can also help in identifying code errors and suggesting fixes.

ix. **Other applications** – GenAI can perform a wide range of tasks, including drafting articles, creating music, generating images and videos, coding, interview preparation, parenting advice, website creation, data analysis, taking minutes of the meeting, and making presentations. Select an appropriate AI tool based on your specific needs.

Before you begin doing anything manually, think AI.

The journey of leveraging GenAI for career advancement is not just about adopting modern technologies but also about cultivating a mindset of continuous learning, agility, innovation, and openness to change. Embrace the opportunities presented by GenAI and pave the way for a future where human potential and artificial intelligence converge to redefine professional excellence.

Note: While GenAI is a technology which is freely accessible, be mindful to use it as per your organization policies. Do not share personal data or company confidential information on open-source platforms as it could lead to data breach resulting in legal issues, financial losses and damage to the organization's reputation.

Also, while open source GenAI technologies may evolve rapidly in a brief period of time, it is not yet a complete replacement to humans, at least as of now. They lack context and can generate outputs that appear plausible but are not factual or based on data. Therefore, be sure to check and validate your work before putting it to final use. Having said that, the pace at which this technology is advancing is unprecedented, and it will not be surprizing if GenAI gets significantly better each year for the next couple of years.

Self-Reflection

i.   *How am I currently using GenAI to be more productive?*

ii. *How can I use GenAI more often to focus more on strategic and value-adding work?*

SUMMARY

As you arrive at this culminating chapter after immersing yourself in the comprehensive exploration of Career Essentials, you are now ready to reflect on the various insights gained from the diverse topics covered throughout the book.

From the foundational understanding of organizational dynamics explored in "Deciphering Organizational Landscape" to the nuanced strategies for strategic thinking elucidated in "Thinking Strategically," each chapter has contributed to your understanding of career success. You have delved into the intricacies of technical and functional proficiency in "Building Technical and Functional Skills," embraced the imperative of a proactive mindset in "Being Proactive," and honed your customer-centric approach in "Elevating Customer Experiences."

Reflecting on your journey, you are reminded of the significance of quality excellence, timely action, and ownership and accountability in driving meaningful results, as expounded upon in "Pursuing Quality Excellence," "The Art of Timeliness," and "Thriving with Ownership and Accountability." You have embraced the power of feedback in "Embracing Feedback" and of innovation in "Unleashing Creativity and Innovation," and honed your interpersonal skills in "Unlocking Collective Potential through Collaboration" and "Navigating the Communication Landscape." You also considered looking beyond performance in "Crafting Your Professional Persona" and using newer technologies in professional setting in "Leveraging GenAI for Career Advancement."

As you synthesize your learnings, it is essential to recognize that the applicability of these topics may vary depending on the culture of your organization. Cultural nuances, organizational structures, and leadership styles all influence how these principles are perceived and practiced within different workplace environments. Therefore, it is crucial to adapt and contextualize these insights to align with the specific dynamics of your organization. Armed with a comprehensive toolkit of skills and strategies, you are now poised to craft your professional persona and navigate your career with confidence and purpose, ready to embrace the challenges and opportunities that lie ahead.

CONCLUSION

As you close *Career Essentials: A Practical Guide to Building a Strong Foundation for Professional Growth*, I hope you carry with you a profound sense of empowerment and a treasure trove of practical wisdom. The journey you have undertaken, guided by these pages, is just the first step towards a successful career.

Remember that the path ahead will be marked by both triumphs and trials. In every challenge, there is an opportunity for growth, and in every accomplishment, a platform for even greater achievements. Your career is an evolving story, and it is yours to shape.

Stay curious and open to learning, for in the world of work, knowledge is an invaluable currency. Build valuable relationships and forge meaningful connections with colleagues and mentors, for they will enrich your journey in ways you cannot yet foresee. Cultivate the essential skills of adaptability, resilience, and emotional intelligence, for these qualities will be your pillars of strength.

The habits and attributes you have developed through these pages will be fundamental to your success. Remember to remain authentic, true to your values, and passionate in your pursuits.

It is my sincere wish that this book serves as a lifelong companion, offering guidance and inspiration as you progress in your career. The initial stages of your career are just the beginning. As you venture forward, be bold, take risks, and chase your aspirations with unwavering determination.

Your career story has just begun. It is a narrative of growth, resilience, and achievement, waiting for you to pen the next chapter. Write it with vigor, guided by the insights you have gathered here, and let your journey be one of enduring success. Your future is brimming with possibilities, and it is yours to create!

With warm regards,

Rahul

CASE SCENARIOS

This segment includes few pseudonymized, real-life scenarios designed to allow you to apply and implement some of the concepts covered in this book. These situations are common challenges you may encounter in the early stages of your career. However, if you are unable to relate to these scenarios, do not worry. It is just a matter of time that you will encounter a comparable situation. Thinking of how you could manage this scenario could help you prepare for when the situation actually occurs.

All names provided in the case scenarios are fictitious. Any resemblance to anyone is purely coincidental.

CASE 1

Thomas has been working with a customer for about a year now. He has been delivering with quality on time over the year. It was CSAT (Customer Satisfaction) survey time and Thomas was expecting a good CSAT score. To his astonishment, while the scores were good on quality and timeliness, the scores on proactivity and responsiveness were low. He wondered if proactivity and responsiveness were not linked to the excellent quality of his work and on time delivery.

What do you think could be the reasons for Thomas getting low scores on proactivity and responsiveness? What would you recommend him to improve his scores on those parameters?

CASE 2

It is the end of the quarter and Melissa is remarkably busy with her deliverables. There is a deluge of requests in her inbox in addition to her regular deliverables. She takes them up one by one and delivers to the satisfaction of the customer.

What risks do you foresee for Melissa? What would be your suggestions to Melissa to create and maintain a positive customer experience in this situation?

CASE 3

Rajiv requests the data from the customer to begin working on a report. The deadline for the report is 3 weeks from now. Rajiv receives the data 1 week after he requested for it which leaves him with 2 weeks to deliver the report. He is able to complete the analysis in 1 week and planning to perform a quality check and make a presentation in the next 1 week. While performing quality check, Rajiv notices that some numbers in the final analysis do not make sense. He performs a deeper analysis and finds that the issue is in the data shared by the customer.

What would be your recommendation to Rajiv to handle this situation? What would you recommend to Rajiv to minimize the chances of this happening again?

CASE 4

Cindy is working on an ad-hoc customer request. She has multiple other requests at hand. Besides work, she is an active participant in other office events and initiatives. While everything was going right in her analysis, a few of the final numbers in her report looked weird to her. Project delivery is due in 2 days. She was planning to perform quality check and submit the final report in these 2 days. She is not sure of what the error could be and how much time it could take to resolve. She is apprehensive if she will be able to deliver the report in time. Being a close friend, she has reached out to you for advice.

What would be your suggestions to Cindy in this situation?

CASE 5

Amyra joined her current organization 3 years back. Since then, she has been working on the same project. While she is doing very well in her current projects, she feels that her learning and growth has stagnated. She sees other team members work on a variety of projects and feels left behind.

What recommendations would you have for Amyra to help her?

CASE 6

Justin is leading five team members on a project supporting 10 countries for a client. There is an issue in one of the deliverables in the month of May for one country. While he is working on actions to avoid recurrence of the issue, another similar issue happens in the month of July for the same country.

How would you suggest Justin to handle this situation?

ACKNOWLEDGEMENTS

I want to express my heartfelt gratitude to all the wonderful people who have played a significant role in shaping my professional journey.

First and foremost, I thank my early mentors, who served as invaluable guides, offering insights and unwavering support as I navigated the initial stages of my career. I am also deeply grateful to my first manager for the tremendous support extended during those formative years.

I am inspired by the great leaders I have had the privilege to work with. Their remarkable leadership continues to motivate not just me, but many others.

A special thanks goes to all my team members for their understanding and relentless support throughout my career. Your contributions have enriched my experiences, and I owe my ability to quote examples in this book to you.

I also extend my gratitude to Harvey Coleman for granting permission to reference the P.I.E. framework in this book.

Finally, to my family - my parents, wife, and children - thank you for your unwavering support. I would not be who I am today, nor would this book have been possible, without you.